THE NEW ENGLAND
CATCH
A Seafood Cookbook

THE NEW ENGLAND
CATCH

A Seafood Cookbook

Martha Watson Murphy

To Betty
with love
Martha
11/3/18

Globe
Pequot

GUILFORD, CONNECTICUT

To
Kevin Ian Murphy
and
all the others who have gone down to the sea in ships

They that go down to the sea in ships,

that do business in great waters:

These see the works of the Lord,

and his wonders in the deep.

—Psalm 107

Globe Pequot

An imprint of The Rowman & Littlefield Publishing Group, Inc.
4501 Forbes Blvd., Ste. 200
Lanham, MD 20706
www.rowman.com

Distributed by NATIONAL BOOK NETWORK

Photos by Al Weems Photographer with the exception of the following:
p. 32 © Brent Hofacker/Shutterstock.com; p. 31 © istockphoto.com/
LauriPatterson; p. 173 © VisFineArt/Shutterstock.com;
All black and white photos from the Library of Congress.

British Library Cataloguing in Publication Information available

Library of Congress Cataloging-in-Publication Data available

ISBN 978-1-4930-1932-8 (hardcover)

ISBN 978-1-4930-1933-5 (e-book)

♾™ The paper used in this publication meets the minimum
requirements of American National Standard for Information
Sciences—Permanence of Paper for Printed Library Materials,
ANSI/NISO Z39.48-1992

Printed in the United States of America

Contents

Introduction

During the first few years of my marriage, my husband was a commercial fisherman. Back then, whenever I'd find myself about to meet someone for the first time, I would dread the moment when the conversation might turn to the subject of our spouses. The revelation that my husband was a commercial fisherman invariably drew a look of surprise or a stunned silence. But in my heart of hearts I was as shocked as anyone to find myself married to a fisherman. After all, commercial fishing is a world of manual labor and macho men, big on brawn and short on brains, isn't it? Why would I want to have anything to do with it?

The stereotypes are partly true—commercial fishing *is* a place for macho men and misfits (terms I use with complete affection), and anyone who wants to hide out from society at large. If you're willing and able, all comers are welcome to try this backbreaking, risky line of work.

You probably don't know any commercial fishermen. Most of us don't. They work on the water while the rest of us spend our days on firm ground. They work all hours of the day (and any day of the year the weather and quotas allow them to fish), while we work nine to five, weekends off. They come and go from fishing ports where, unless you're in a business that repairs or supplies the boats, you're not likely to ever go.

I was introduced to this mysterious world shortly after I started dating the man who would later become my husband (actually, when we met, he was building custom boats). It wasn't long before I wanted to tell others about this interesting business and quirky group of people. It seemed only natural to do that by writing a seafood cookbook—it's *food*, after all, that commercial fishermen provide to us. (Plus, I love cookbooks.) It seemed everyone I knew—even good cooks—were confounded by the thought of cooking seafood at home: "I love seafood—it's what I always order when we eat out—but I don't know how to cook it," was something I heard over and over. Aha! I would show them how to cook delicious seafood dishes, *and* give them a glimpse into the world of fishing!

What attracts a person to commercial fishing? Certainly the physical environment is part of it; "being out on the water" is always mentioned when fishermen are asked what they like about their jobs. Fishing also offers a way to "get away from it all"—the rest of us and the petty hassles of everyday life ashore. I believe a lot of people who fish for a living have chosen fishing, at least partially, for this reason. One of the trade-offs, though, is a schedule that is unpredictable from day to day, making it hard to find partners who will put up with that part of the bargain.

The two other most frequently mentioned reasons for wanting to go fishing are being one's own boss (even crew are "self-employed") and the satisfaction that comes from meeting the challenges of the job. Certainly most of us can understand the appeal of independence, but it has a cost: Fishermen have no guaranteed income. And the challenges that fishermen love meeting would drive most people crazy: working in an environment that is dangerous and unpredictable, and figuring out how to bring back a commodity that remains hidden from view until the net or trap is aboard—and for prices that fluctuate as wildly as the stock market. Surviving and thriving in this business requires physical strength and mental acuity in equal measures.

These traits—a love of the sea, an independent spirit, and an enjoyment of physical work—are shared by most fishermen, despite any differences in background and education. Don't think of them as a "group," however; most of them tend to be loners rather than team players.

As I investigated the history of commercial fishing in New England for the original edition of this book, I was fascinated to learn that it was of crucial economic importance to the early colonists and to the funding of the Revolutionary War. By the late nineteenth century the fishing schooners of Gloucester, Massa-

"We used to haul in by hand. If you had 10,000 pounds of butterfish, you'd haul until you couldn't haul no more, and then the boat would roll and you'd pinch it against the rails and pull it up some more when the boat rolled back. Then when you'd get to the cod end, we'd hook the whip to it and lift it in. Four guys could pull in a net of 10,000 pounds. I wouldn't still be fishing without net drums. People used to retire in their fifties unless they were the captain."

—a fisherman from Narragansett, Rhode Island

chusetts, made up the most successful fishing fleet in the world. The state of Maine is still the nation's largest supplier of fresh lobster.

As you may know, New England fishermen today face more restrictions than even before. There is disagreement between fishermen and scientists as to whether certain species have been "overfished" or not, and there is great disagreement between fishermen and the government on how to address the problems. Some fishermen do not admit to any serious changes in the stocks at all, saying that fish populations are cyclical, while others who do admit declines in populations blame them on pollution, or fisheries other than the one in which they participate: Gillnetters blame draggermen, draggermen blame gillnetters, and 'round and 'round it goes.

It is not my purpose in this book to take a stand on the issues of fishing and government regulations. I believe that fishermen and commercial fishing will find a way to carry on as long as we have oceans and the hardy souls eager to venture out on them.

The recipes in this book are meant to encourage you to try a variety of seafood in a variety of ways. Many of these recipes are my own invention (when my husband was a fisherman, there was a steady supply of seafood coming through the door and I had to do something with it). Others are ones I've adapted from miscellaneous sources over the years; those are credited to the originator.

The old saying "There is nothing new under the sun" is true, especially when it comes to recipes, but I hope you'll find a collection here that *is* new to you, and one you'll turn to again and again. I am confident that you can reproduce these dishes in your own kitchen to rave reviews from family and friends.

I hope this book will also provide you with a look inside the world of commercial fishing—who the fishermen are and how the seafood on your plate got there. I hope it will give you a new respect for the men and women who go down to the sea in ships. This book is my tribute to them—the ones out there today and all who have gone before.

Help keep the tradition of commercial fishing going by buying seafood, and help yourself by eating it. Adding more wild-caught seafood to your diet is a smart, delicious, healthy way to eat!

Martha W. Murphy

CHAPTER 1

Starters

Recipes

Smoked Bluefish Pâté

Crab and Roasted Red Pepper Dip

Clams Casino

Garlic Shrimp

Smoked Salmon with
Herbed Cheese Spread

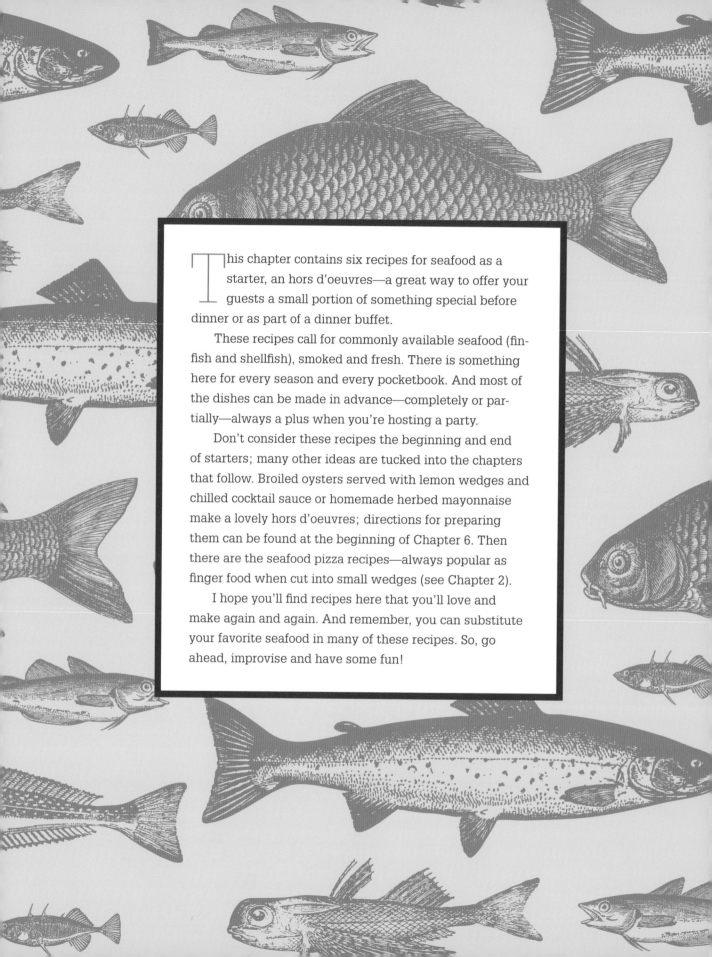

This chapter contains six recipes for seafood as a starter, an hors d'oeuvres—a great way to offer your guests a small portion of something special before dinner or as part of a dinner buffet.

These recipes call for commonly available seafood (finfish and shellfish), smoked and fresh. There is something here for every season and every pocketbook. And most of the dishes can be made in advance—completely or partially—always a plus when you're hosting a party.

Don't consider these recipes the beginning and end of starters; many other ideas are tucked into the chapters that follow. Broiled oysters served with lemon wedges and chilled cocktail sauce or homemade herbed mayonnaise make a lovely hors d'oeuvres; directions for preparing them can be found at the beginning of Chapter 6. Then there are the seafood pizza recipes—always popular as finger food when cut into small wedges (see Chapter 2).

I hope you'll find recipes here that you'll love and make again and again. And remember, you can substitute your favorite seafood in many of these recipes. So, go ahead, improvise and have some fun!

Smoked Bluefish Pâté

Smoked fish makes a great hors d'oeuvre on its own but for variety it is wonderful made up as a pâté. Here, smoked bluefish is paired with caramelized onions and mushrooms, herbs, brandy, and goat cheese. Rich and flavorful, it spreads well on rye toasts, crackers, or endive—a great start to an evening. You can also prepare it in advance and add it to your picnic basket with a loaf of crusty bread and a bunch of red grapes. This recipe can also be made with smoked mackerel.

Makes about 2 cups of pâté

1 tablespoon oil

1 tablespoon butter

3/4 cup chopped onion

1 cup sliced mushrooms

2 peppercorns

1 whole clove

1 bay leaf

3 juniper berries, crushed (optional)

1/4 cup brandy

1/2 pound smoked bluefish (or smoked mackerel)

5 ounces goat cheese (or cream cheese)

2 tablespoons light cream

In a large, heavy skillet heat the oil and butter over medium heat. Add the onion, mushrooms, and spices, and cook, stirring occasionally, until the vegetables are tender and have golden brown edges. Pour in the brandy and continue to cook until the liquid has reduced by half. Remove from the heat, and when cool enough to touch, remove and discard the bay leaf and clove.

Place the vegetable mixture in the bowl of a food processor. Pull the skin off the bluefish and add it in chunks to the vegetables. Add the cheese, in bits, and the cream. Pulse to blend completely, scraping down the side of the bowl with a spatula a couple of times. When the mixture is smooth, transfer it to a small serving dish; cover and chill for at least 1 hour before serving.

*Note: For a chunky pâté, reserve some of the caramelized vegetables to stir into the pâté after it has been blended.

When fishermen are asked what they like about fishing, they always mention the physical beauty of the ocean and the opportunity to be out on it for long silent stretches, and "doing what I want, when I want, and how I want."

Crab and Roasted Red Pepper Dip

This "dip" is versatile! Use it to top cooked whole artichoke hearts (chilled) for a first course; pile it into a ripe avocado for a special luncheon; smear it over crisp bruschetta for party food; or put it out with pita chips for dipping. Try it once and you'll find many more uses for it.

Makes about 3 cups

½ pound cooked lump crabmeat

2 cups sour cream

1 red bell pepper, roasted, skin and seeds removed, and chopped (about ⅔ cup) (see below)

2 tablespoons chopped fresh basil

1 clove garlic, pressed

¼ cup chopped scallion

Salt and pepper to taste

Combine all ingredients well in a large bowl. Cover and refrigerate for at least 1 hour before serving to allow flavors to develop. Remove from refrigerator 10 minutes before using so that the mixture is not ice cold.

How to Roast Peppers

Wash the peppers and place them, whole and barely touching, on a cookie sheet or in a shallow pan. Set under a hot broiler, 4–6 inches from the flame. Turn occasionally with tongs and broil until the skin is completely blackened.

Place the roasted peppers in a brown paper bag, close the top, and let them cool for a few minutes. When the peppers are cool enough to handle, pinch and lift off the charred skin (it will come away easily), working over a bowl to catch any juices (save for the recipe, if needed, or add to a salad dressing if desired). Discard the blackened skin, then halve the peppers and remove and discard the seeds. The roasted peppers are now ready to be used in any recipe that calls for them.

Roasted peppers can be stored in the refrigerator for a day or two before using.

Clams Casino

Served in the shell, this dish makes a pretty presentation as well as a tasty party food. Allow about 4 per person as a first course or as an item in a buffet. The bacon is the perfect partner to the flavor of the clams.

Makes 24 clams casino

24 live littleneck or cherry stone clams

¼ cup finely minced onion

⅛ cup finely minced green bell pepper

⅛ cup finely minced sweet red bell pepper

2 tablespoons chopped fresh parsley

½ cup dried bread crumbs, or cracker crumbs

2 tablespoons olive oil

Lemon juice, or white wine

4 slices of bacon, cut into 24 small pieces

Lemon wedges

Set oven temperature to 450°F.

Scrub the clams under cold running water to remove any grit from the shells. Open the clams with a clam knife, working over a bowl to catch juices. (Strain and reserve any juices that accumulate in the bowl.) Once the clams are open, use the knife to loosen the clam meat attached to the shell (leaving the meat sitting in that half of the shell).

Arrange the clams (on the half-shell) on a cookie sheet; set aside.

In a mixing bowl combine the minced vegetables, parsley, bread or cracker crumbs, and olive oil. Add the strained clam juice, and a small spritz of fresh lemon juice or white wine (barely a teaspoon). Mix to combine thoroughly.

Carefully place equal amounts of the topping on each raw clam. Top that with a piece of bacon. At this point, you can cover and refrigerate the clams until ready to cook.

Place the tray of clams in a preheated oven and bake for 10 minutes or until the bacon is cooked. Finish under the broiler for a crisper top, if desired—watch closely so they do not burn! Serve piping hot, with lemon wedges and small forks on the side.

Garlic Shrimp

This easy-to-make and delicious shrimp appetizer will dress up any party table. More good news: You can marinate the shrimp the night before and finish up the recipe in 30 minutes.

Serves 8

5 tablespoons mayonnaise

1/2 teaspoon black pepper

5 tablespoons lemon juice

4 garlic cloves, minced

2 pounds raw large shrimp, shelled* and deveined

1 cup whole grain bread crumbs

1 teaspoon crushed dried basil

2 tablespoons melted butter

In a medium-size bowl, combine mayonnaise, pepper, lemon juice and garlic; stir until well blended.

Place shrimp in a large shallow glass dish. Pour marinade over shrimp, toss until evenly coated with marinade and cover the dish tightly with plastic wrap. Store in refrigerator for a minimum of 4 hours or overnight.

Place a sheet of parchment paper in a large shallow baking pan. In a small bowl, combine bread crumbs and basil.

Remove the shrimp from the refrigerator and drain, reserving half the marinade in a bowl. Coat each shrimp with bread crumbs; place in a single layer on the parchment paper. Add the melted butter to the reserved marinade, stir, and using a small spoon dribble a little of the mixture over each shrimp until all of it is used.

Bake for 20 minutes, or until opaque. Serve immediately.

Note: When you remove the shells from the shrimp, leave them intact at the tail; it adds flavor and makes it easy to pick up the shrimp to eat out of hand if you serve this as an hors d'oeuvre (and at a party, it makes a great one).

Smoked Salmon with Herbed Cheese Spread

Here, toasted slices of a baguette are spread with goat cheese and fresh herbs, then topped with cucumber, smoked salmon, and fresh dill. You can assemble a platter just before your guests arrive; then, remove from the fridge, squeeze fresh lemon juice over the top, and serve.

Buy smoked salmon that has already been sliced. The recipe works just as well with cream cheese if you don't like goat cheese.

Serves 10

FOR THE CHEESE SPREAD:

10 ounces goat cheese (or cream cheese)

2 tablespoons softened butter

2 tablespoons finely chopped flat leaf parsley

2 tablespoons finely chopped scallions

1 tablespoon chopped fresh dill

½ teaspoon freshly ground black pepper

FOR THE TOASTS:

1 loaf of long slender crusty bread, thinly sliced

2–3 tablespoons olive oil

1½ pounds smoked salmon

1 English cucumber, peeled and thinly sliced

1 bunch of fresh dill

2 lemons, cut in wedges

To make the cheese spread: In a medium bowl combine all the ingredients well with a fork. Cover and refrigerate until ready to use.

To make the toasts: Slice the bread in generous ¼-inch slices. Brush both sides with a little oil and place under the broiler—watch closely! Toast each side until golden. Transfer to a rack to cool completely.

To assemble: Spread each cooled toast with some of the herbed cheese mixture. Place a paper-thin slice of cucumber on the cheese and top that with a thin slice of smoked salmon. Place a small sprig of dill on the salmon; squeeze lemon juice over all. Serve immediately.

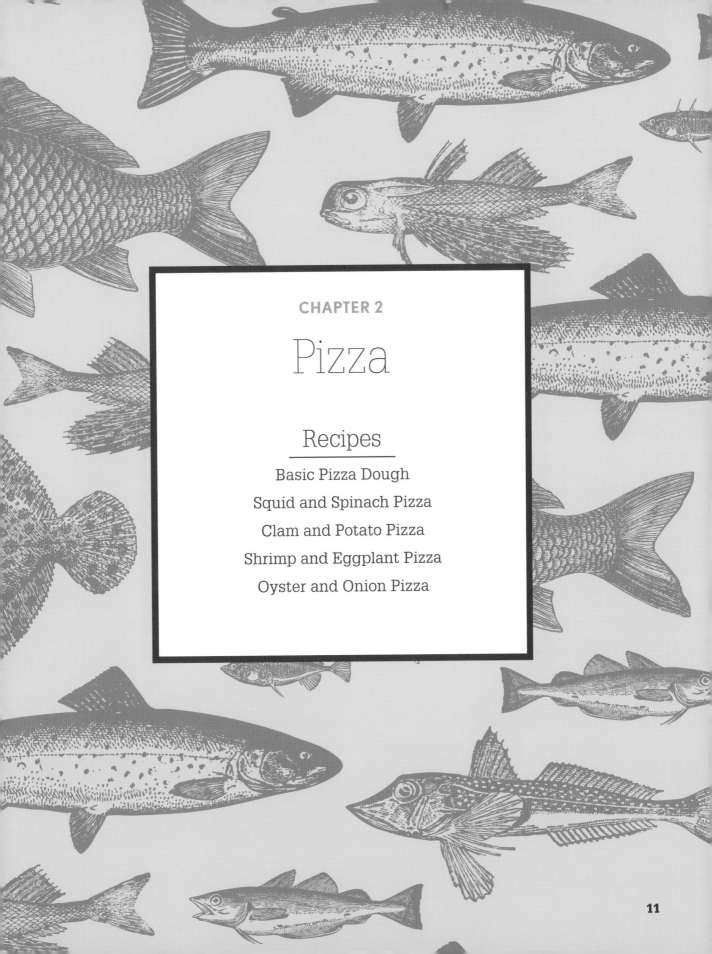

CHAPTER 2

Pizza

Recipes

Basic Pizza Dough

Squid and Spinach Pizza

Clam and Potato Pizza

Shrimp and Eggplant Pizza

Oyster and Onion Pizza

Pizza, it turns out, is not "junk food" after all. A wholesome crust topped with fresh herbs and vegetables and a little meat and cheese is a healthful meal. Add a crisp green salad, and you have dinner. Cut into small squares or triangles, pizzas also make fabulous finger foods for a party. The four recipes here will show you how to make delicious pizzas using seafood instead of sausage or pepperoni—yum!

To keep things simple, you can buy pizza dough at the supermarket (it's usually packaged in bags and kept in the dairy section). Or, for even better flavor, make your own with the Basic Pizza Dough recipe.

The possibilities for seafood pizzas are far greater than this handful of recipes. Try lump crabmeat with fresh corn kernels and Fontina cheese. Or smoked mackerel with apples and Gorgonzola cheese. You will soon come up with your own combinations—enjoy!

Basic Pizza Dough

1 package dry yeast (2¹/₂ teaspoons)

¹/₂ teaspoon sugar

²/₃ cup warm water

2 tablespoons olive oil

2 cups unbleached white flour (King Arthur is best)

¹/₂ teaspoon salt

Place the yeast, sugar, and ⅓ cup of warm water in a large bowl and stir to dissolve. Let sit for 10 minutes. Add the remaining ⅓ cup of water, olive oil, flour, and salt, and blend well. Form the dough into a ball, place on a floured board, and knead until smooth and elastic—about 5 minutes.

Form the dough into a ball and place it in a large lightly oiled bowl. Turn the dough once so that it is lightly oiled on all sides. Cover the bowl with a clean dish towel and leave in a warm place for 1 hour. The dough should double in size. Punch it down and roll it out on a lightly floured board to use immediately or wrap well in plastic wrap and refrigerate until ready to use.

You can add chopped fresh herbs, finely minced or pressed garlic, or grated Parmesan cheese to the pizza dough for added flavor, if you like.

Making Pizza Dough

When making pizza dough, you can mix the ingredients by hand in a large bowl or in a food processor fitted with the dough blade. Either way, there is a little kneading required before letting the dough rise. It needs to rise for one hour but can then be refrigerated until you are ready to use it. Pizza dough will keep in the refrigerator for at least a week, so make a double batch and store half for later use.

Shaping Pizza Dough

Place the dough on a board sprinkled with a little flour. Using your hands or a rolling pin, flatten the ball of dough. Flour your hands or the rolling pin and, starting in the center of the dough, push down and out. It will be springy and will tend to pull back into a smaller shape than you've made. Once you have the dough in the shape and thickness you want, let it sit for fifteen minutes. Then, if necessary, stretch the dough again before topping.

Using a Pizza Stone

You can bake your pizza on a pizza stone, pizza pan, cookie sheet, or jelly roll pan. If you are using a metal pan, always give it a thin wipe of olive oil and then a sprinkle of cornmeal before laying the crust on it. With a stone, just a sprinkle of cornmeal is necessary to keep the dough from sticking and to produce a crispy crust. Preheating the stone for 15 minutes in a hot oven will give you an even crisper crust.

Fishing in New England has more often than not been a family endeavor. Even when an older member is no longer able to go out on the boats, he can play an important role shoreside—repairing gear, buying supplies, and seeing to the many other details required in the business. This support can help the younger generation tremendously, allowing them to focus more on the actual work of fishing.

Squid and Spinach Pizza

Squid is plentiful and inexpensive, and this pizza is a good way to try it if you've never had it before. Here, squid rings and tentacles top a pizza along with fresh spinach, red peppers, and feta cheese. The spinach keeps its deep green color, the peppers stay bright red, and the squid and feta are creamy white, making this pizza as pretty as it is tasty.

Makes one 12-inch to 14-inch round pizza

FOR THE CRUST:

2½ tablespoons olive oil

1 teaspoon cornmeal, for pizza pan

**1 batch Basic Pizza Dough (page 13)
or one bag of dough from market**

FOR THE TOPPING:

½ cup tomato sauce

1 tablespoon anchovy paste

2 garlic cloves, finely minced or pressed

4 cups fresh baby spinach

½ cup loosely packed whole basil leaves

**¾ pound cleaned squid (see page 177),
cut into ¼-inch rings**

**2 large red bell peppers, roasted, peeled,
and seeded (see page 5)**

½ pound feta cheese

¼ cup grated Parmesan cheese

Preheat oven to 450°F

Prepare the pizza pan by wiping the surface with a little olive oil and sprinkling with cornmeal; a pizza stone needs cornmeal only. Roll out the dough and lay it on the pan or stone, crimping and shaping the edge to desired thickness. Brush the dough with 1 tablespoon of olive oil.

In a small bowl mix the tomato sauce with the anchovy paste and garlic. Spread over the pizza dough, starting ½ inch in from the edge.

Evenly distribute the spinach over the tomato sauce. Chop the basil coarsely and sprinkle over the spinach.

Distribute the squid rings (and tentacles, if you are using them) evenly over the spinach and basil.

Cut the roasted peppers into long narrow strips and then into ½-inch sections. Distribute evenly over the pizza. Crumble the feta cheese and sprinkle over the pizza; follow with the Parmesan cheese.

Drizzle a tablespoon of olive oil over the pizza, concentrating on the squid pieces, and then a pinch of salt and freshly ground black pepper.

Bake for about 20 minutes, or until the crust is done, the squid is white, and the top of the pizza is steaming hot. Cut and serve immediately.

In the days of schooner fishing, shipwrecks were not the only dangers facing fishermen at sea. Some of the dorymen never made it back to the ship; some fell out of the rigging, were struck by booms, or were washed overboard by high seas.

Clam and Potato Pizza

Potatoes on a pizza may sound odd but when sliced paper thin they become a tender bed beneath the rest of the toppings—and a perfect backdrop to the flavors of the clams, bacon, and onions.

To save time, buy minced clams at your fish market or, if you prefer, buy littlenecks in the shell and cook them at home. (If you do, you'll also end up with some broth to add to your fish stock collection.) If you buy minced clams, three-quarters of a pound is enough for this pizza.

Makes one 12-inch to 14-inch round pizza

FOR THE CRUST:

2 ½ tablespoons olive oil

1 teaspoon cornmeal, for pizza pan

1 batch Basic Pizza Dough (page 13) or 1 bag of dough
    from the market

FOR THE TOPPING:

3 dozen littleneck clams in the shell, cleaned and
    steamed (see page 106)

4 slices lean bacon

³/₄ pound potatoes (2 medium-size potatoes)

Salt and freshly ground black pepper

1 medium onion, cut into thin slivers (about ²/₃ cup)

1 tablespoon finely chopped fresh parsley

2 teaspoons finely chopped fresh marjoram

3 tablespoons grated Parmesan cheese

1 tablespoon olive oil

Preheat oven to 450°F.

Prepare the pizza pan by wiping the surface with olive oil and sprinkling with cornmeal; a pizza stone needs cornmeal only. Roll out the dough and lay it on the pan or stone, crimping and shaping the edge to the desired thickness. Brush the dough with 1 tablespoon of olive oil.

If you are cooking fresh clams: When the clams are cool enough to handle, remove the meat and set aside. If the clams are very small, leave them whole; otherwise chop them coarsely.

Cut the bacon into 1-inch chunks and cook in a skillet over medium heat until it has rendered fat but has not become crisp. Use a slotted spoon to remove the bacon from the skillet and set aside.

Using a food processor fitted with the slicing disc, cut the potatoes into paper-thin slices. Arrange the slices in overlapping circles over the pizza dough, starting ½ inch from the outside edge. Sprinkle a small amount of salt and pepper over the potatoes. Next, evenly distribute the bacon over the potatoes, then the clams (drain the clams if you are using already-minced from the market), then the onion. Sprinkle the pizza with the herbs and Parmesan cheese, and drizzle a tablespoon of olive oil over all.

Bake for about 20 minutes, or until the crust is done, the potatoes are tender, the bacon is crisp, and the top of the pizza is steaming hot. Cut and serve immediately.

Shrimp and Eggplant Pizza

The exquisite combination of shrimp, roasted eggplant, fresh basil, and goat cheese make this pizza a standout. The eggplant can be prepared a few hours in advance.

Makes one 12-inch to 14-inch pizza

FOR THE CRUST:

Olive oil for wiping pan and brushing dough

1 teaspoon cornmeal, for pizza pan

1 batch Basic Pizza Dough (page 13) or 1 bag of dough from the market

FOR THE TOPPING:

1 large eggplant (about 1¼–1½ pounds)

5 tablespoons olive oil

¾ pound medium shrimp, shelled and deveined

1 garlic clove, pressed

½ cup tomato sauce

¼ cup grated Asiago cheese

½ cup goat cheese (or Feta cheese)

2 tablespoons finely chopped fresh basil

1 tablespoon finely chopped fresh flat leaf parsley

Preheat oven to 450°F.

Prepare the pizza pan by wiping the surface with olive oil and sprinkling with cornmeal; a pizza stone needs cornmeal only. Roll out the dough and lay it on the pan or stone, crimping and shaping the edge to desired thickness. Brush the dough with 1 tablespoon of olive oil.

Prepare the eggplant: Cut the eggplant lengthwise into ¼- to ⅜-inch slices. Brush with 4 tablespoons of olive oil and place on a jelly roll pan. Cook under a broiler, turning once, until golden on both sides—3–5 minutes per side. Remove pan to a cooling rack.

In a large bowl toss the shrimp with the garlic and remaining tablespoon of olive oil. Cover and set aside.

Starting ½ inch in from the edge, spread the tomato sauce over the oiled pizza dough. Cut the broiled eggplant slices into 1-inch strips and then cut the strips into 1-inch pieces. Distribute evenly over the sauce, adding any juices that have formed in the pan. Sprinkle half of the Asiago cheese over the eggplant. Next, evenly distribute the shrimp over the eggplant, and top with the rest of the Asiago cheese. Place little pieces of goat cheese (or Feta cheese) over all and sprinkle with the herbs. Drizzle any garlic oil left from the shrimp marinade over all, and sprinkle with a pinch of salt and freshly ground black pepper.

Bake for about 20 minutes, or until the crust is done, the shrimp are cooked, and the top of the pizza is steaming hot. Cut and serve immediately.

Oyster and Onion Pizza

This pizza calls for few ingredients but each has such a distinctive flavor their combination is a good example of "less is more." The onion cooks down into a savory bed for the oysters, and both are complemented by two flavorful cheeses.

Makes one 12-inch to 14-inch round pizza

FOR THE CRUST:

Olive oil for wiping pan

1 teaspoon cornmeal, for pizza pan

1 batch Basic Pizza Dough (page 13) or 1 bag of dough from the market

FOR THE TOPPING:

2 garlic cloves, finely minced or pressed

2 tablespoons olive oil

3 tablespoons crumbled Gorgonzola cheese

3 medium onions, sliced extremely thin

³/₄ pound shucked raw oysters, drained (liquid reserved) and coarsely chopped

¹/₄ cup grated Asiago cheese

1 tablespoon finely chopped fresh flat leaf parsley

1 teaspoon finely chopped fresh thyme

Preheat oven to 450°F.

Prepare the pizza pan by wiping the surface with olive oil and sprinkling with cornmeal; a pizza stone needs only cornmeal. Roll out the dough and lay it on the pan or stone, crimping and shaping the edge to desired thickness.

In a small bowl combine the garlic with 1 tablespoon of olive oil and spread over the pizza dough. Sprinkle the Gorgonzola evenly over the dough ½ inch in from the edge. Arrange the onions over the cheese in overlapping circles. Evenly distribute the drained oysters (save the liquid for fish stock) over the onions; season with a pinch of salt and freshly ground black pepper. Sprinkle with the Asiago cheese, parsley, and thyme. Drizzle the remaining tablespoon of olive oil over all.

Bake for about 20 minutes, or until the crust is done, the onions are tender, the oysters are cooked, and the top of the pizza is steaming hot. Cut and serve immediately.

This scene used to be a common sight when nets were made of natural fibers. The nets had to be hung up to dry to prevent rotting. This was also a handy way to mend a net. Nowadays, nets are made of synthetic fibers that resist rotting, and the need for drying racks has virtually disappeared.

Chowders and Soups

Recipes

In this chapter you'll find chowders and velvety soups that call for virtually any finfish or shellfish you like. These recipes are perfect for lunch or a soup course at dinner, and are also suitable as a main course.

To make a good soup from scratch you will need a large stockpot (stainless steel is best) or a Dutch oven (these are made of cast iron or of enameled cast iron and can be used on top of the stove or in the oven), a colander, a fine-mesh sieve, and cheesecloth (hardware stores and kitchen supply stores sell cheesecloth).

You can buy good commercially prepared fish stock these days but, if you can find the time, I recommend that you make your own. You won't believe how easy it is, and you will end up with a superior product. Fish stock is made by cooking fish "racks" (the body of the fish after it is filleted) and/or shellfish shells with a combination of vegetables ("aromatics" as they are called), herbs, water, and wine. Stock forms the base for seafood soups and chowders, and can also be used as the base for making seafood sauces and risotto.

If you're not experienced at soup-making, start with the Oven-Baked Fish Chowder (page 29); it's the easiest recipe in this chapter and it's so good the results will make you feel like a professional chef! Add some good bread and a salad, and you have a healthful, satisfying, delicious dinner.

"Men who go in for this life are not worrying overmuch about being lost. . . . They would hardly be trying to make a living at bank fishing; at least they would not try for long and surely never at all in winter."

—James B. Connolly, *The Book of Gloucester Fishermen*

Making Fish Stock

There is something satisfying about making fish stock. Perhaps it is the way a handful of simple, homely items—fish bones, some root vegetables, and water—are transformed during the cooking process into a delicate broth of complex flavors.

To make really good stock, get in the habit of saving food scraps that you might normally throw away: the shells of peeled shrimp, fish racks (bones, head, and skin of filleted fish), cooking liquid from steaming shellfish (except lobster; that liquid can be bitter), and vegetable trimmings such as celery leaves and parsley stems. All of these can be stored in the freezer—in airtight packages, labeled and dated—until you are ready to make stock.

The vegetables and herbs used in the making of stock are generally discarded along with the fish parts after the stock is made. (*Sometimes* the vegetables are removed, pureed, and added back to the strained stock, but this is an exception.)

Stock can be kept in your freezer and added to over time if the initial amount is too small for any recipe. It is perfectly fine to combine stocks made from different fish or shellfish; if anything, you'll get an even better result.

If you don't know how to fillet fish and don't want to learn, you can probably get fresh fish carcasses from your local fish market (these are left over from the filleting process). Just ask.

When you get home, freeze the fish carcasses or place them in your stockpot with some water, wine, herbs, and vegetables. Let them simmer while you put away groceries. The finished stock can then be stored in the refrigerator or freezer until you need it.

*Note: Unlike a chicken or beef stock, a longer simmer does not make for a richer fish stock! Too much time can make fish stock unpleasantly strong or bitter-tasting. Thirty minutes is just right. Recipe follows on page 28.

Basic Fish Stock

As a general rule, use 1 quart of water and 1 cup of white wine for each pound and a half of fish parts. Increase or decrease as needed: for example, for 2 pounds of fish parts use 6 cups of water and 1½ cups of wine, etc.

You can use almost any saltwater fish to make a stock except the really oily ones, like mackerel and bluefish. Some cooks recommend using only delicate fish, such as sole, but I find blackfish, sea trout, and cod all make excellent stock. Experiment. And don't be afraid to use more than one kind of fish in your stock.

You can vary this basic stock recipe depending on your taste and what you have on hand. For instance, you can use vermouth instead of wine (but use a bit less); you can use leeks instead of onion; and you can use nearly any fresh herb you like.

Makes about 1 quart

1½ pounds fish carcass (head, tails, bones, and skin)

1 quart water

1 cup dry white wine

1 onion, peeled but left whole

2 whole cloves

1 carrot, split lengthwise

1 stalk celery, split lengthwise

1 bay leaf

¼ teaspoon whole black peppercorns

3 sprigs of fresh flat leaf parsley

Rinse the fish parts under cold running water and place them in a large stockpot. Add the water and wine. Stud the onion with the cloves and add it to the pot along with the rest of the ingredients. Place over high heat and bring to a boil; reduce the heat to a simmer and continue cooking at a low simmer, uncovered, for 30 minutes.

Strain the stock by pouring it through a fine-mesh sieve lined with 2 layers of dampened cheesecloth that is set in a large bowl. Discard all solids. Refrigerate or freeze the stock until ready to use.

Only season the stock with salt and pepper when you are ready to use it in a recipe; the other ingredients will affect its flavor, as will any further reducing of the liquid.

Oven-Baked Fish Chowder

Unlike more traditional recipes for chowder, this does not call for homemade fish stock, rendered salt pork, and hours of straining, tending, and simmering. This recipe is fast and easy—a few staple pantry items are combined with the fish of your choice and then transformed into an exquisite chowder during a leisurely hour in the oven.

This recipe is rich even when made with milk, not light cream. You can also use evaporated milk.

Serves 6

2 pounds cod, haddock, hake,
   or any firm white fish fillets

3 cups diced potatoes

1½ cups diced celery

1½ cups diced onion

1 bay leaf

1 teaspoon salt

4 whole cloves

4 tablespoons butter

1½ teaspoons chopped fresh dill

¼ teaspoon freshly ground black pepper

½ cup dry white wine

2 cups boiling water or fish stock

1 garlic clove, finely minced

1 cup milk or light cream

2 teaspoons chopped fresh flat leaf parsley

Preheat oven to 375°F.

Rub your fingertips along the fish to feel for bones; remove any with tweezers. Place the fish fillets, whole, in a 4-quart Dutch oven or other ovenproof casserole that can be transferred later to the top of the stove. The fish will flake into bite-size pieces as it cooks; do not cut it. Add the vegetables and all the remaining ingredients except the milk (or cream) and parsley to the pot with the fish. Cover, place in the preheated oven and bake for 1 hour.

Transfer the Dutch oven to the top of the stove and set it over low heat. Slowly stir in the milk or cream. Let sit over low heat for 5–10 minutes. Add the fresh parsley and serve immediately.

Remove the cloves if you see them when you ladle out the soup. Make sure your dinner companions know to watch for them if you don't find them all.

Variations:

Follow this recipe as given the first time you make it but after that you may want to improvise. Here are some ideas:

1. Add 1 cup of fresh corn kernels when you add the milk or cream.

2. Cook 3 slices of bacon, drain, and crumble. Sprinkle some over each serving.

3. Substitute fresh tarragon for the dill.

4. Add ½ cup of diced carrots to the ingredients before placing in the oven.

5. Add 1 cup of drained and chopped stewed tomatoes when adding the milk/cream.

Clam Chowder

There is no shortage of recipes for clam chowder. This one is my idea of the quintessential chowder: chock-full of clams and tender potatoes in a flavorful broth. As with any chowder or soup, this is even better the next day.

Serves 6-8

48 live littleneck clams

1 cup water

1½ cups dry white wine

8 tablespoons butter

1½ cups chopped onions

4 cups diced peeled potatoes

½ teaspoon chopped fresh thyme

6 cups milk

Salt and pepper to taste

Scrub the clams with a stiff brush under cold running water to remove any grit from the shells.

Place the water and ½ cup of wine in a large stockpot and bring to a boil. Add the clams in batches of a dozen or more to the pot, depending on its size; cover and cook over high heat for about 5 minutes. As the clams open, remove them from the pot with tongs and set aside in a large bowl. Discard any clams that fail to open. Reserve the cooking liquid.

When you have cooked all the clams and they are cool enough to handle, remove the meat. Work over a bowl to catch any liquid, discarding the shells as you go and placing the clam meat in a separate bowl. Add the juice from the picked clams to the liquid in the stockpot. Set a fine-mesh sieve lined with 2 layers of dampened cheesecloth over a large bowl; strain the stockpot liquid through it. You should have 4–5 cups of liquid. Cover and set aside.

In a Dutch oven or heavy soup pot, melt the butter over medium heat. Add the onions and cook until tender and translucent but not browned. Add the strained clam broth and the remaining cup of wine. Bring to a boil and cook for 5 minutes to intensify the flavors.

Add the potatoes to the pot. When it returns to a boil, lower the heat to a simmer, cover the pot, and cook for about 10 minutes, or until the potatoes are tender but not falling apart.

Add the thyme, clams, and milk to the pot and continue to cook over very low heat, stirring occasionally, until the chowder is heated through; do not allow the chowder to boil at this point. Season to taste with salt and pepper, and serve hot.

Oyster Chowder

A steaming bowl of oyster chowder is the perfect antidote to a long day spent outside in the cold. This hearty chowder is surprisingly quick to assemble and is rich and satisfying. Add some oyster crackers or perhaps some bread warmed from the oven, plus a crisp salad, and you have a complete meal.

Serves 6

½ pound bacon, cooked, drained, and crumbled (with drippings reserved)

3 cups diced potatoes

½ cup diced carrot

1 cup chopped onion

½ cup chopped celery

½ teaspoon salt

½ teaspoon freshly ground black pepper

1 cup water

4 cups milk

1 pint shucked oysters, in liquid

1 tablespoon chopped flat leaf parsley (optional)

6 pats of butter (optional)

Place 3 tablespoons of the bacon drippings in a large soup pot or Dutch oven. Add the potatoes, carrot, onion, and celery, and cook over medium heat. When the potatoes are tender, add the salt, pepper, and water. Bring to a boil, cover, and cook at a simmer for 15 minutes. Add the milk and stir until the mixture returns to a simmer. Add the oysters with their liquid and continue cooking for about 5 minutes, or until the edges of the oysters curl. Ladle into soup bowls, top each with some bacon and parsley (optional) and a pat of butter (optional), and serve immediately.

Seafood Chowder

This chowder starts with rendered salt pork, an old-fashioned technique that adds tremendous flavor. The seafood here is a combination of scallops, quahogs, and monkfish (or any other firm white fish such as cod or haddock). Milk makes a perfectly satisfactory chowder, but for a richer version use light cream.

Serves 8

24 live quahogs (clams)

1 cup water

½ cup dry white wine

¼ pound salt pork

3 cups chopped onions

1 cup chopped celery

2 cups fish stock (homemade or commercially prepared)

3 cups diced potatoes

1 tablespoon chopped fresh parsley

1 bay leaf

½ teaspoon chopped fresh thyme

½ teaspoon chopped fresh marjoram

½ pound shucked scallops

½ pound fish (monkfish, cod, haddock, or other firm white fish), cut in 1-inch cubes

4 cups milk or light cream

1 tablespoon butter

Salt and pepper to taste

Scrub the quahogs under cold running water to remove any grit from the shells. In a large stockpot bring the water and wine to a boil. Add the quahogs, cover, and cook for about 5 minutes, or until the shells open. As they open, remove the clams with tongs and transfer to a large bowl to cool. Discard any clams that do not open. When the clams are cool enough to handle, remove the meat from them. Work over a bowl to catch any liquid, discarding the shells as you go and placing the clam meat in a separate bowl. Add the juice from the picked clams to the liquid in the stockpot. Cover and refrigerate the picked clam meat.

Add any juices that collected from the cooked clams to the cooking liquid in the stockpot. Place over high heat and bring to a boil. Simmer, uncovered, for 5 minutes to reduce it. Place a fine-mesh sieve lined with 2 layers of dampened cheesecloth over a large bowl. Pour the stock through it. Reserve 1 cup to use later in the chowder (the remainder can be added to your stock collection in the freezer).

Cut the salt pork into small cubes and cook, stirring occasionally, in a Dutch oven or soup pot, over medium heat. When the salt pork is golden and crisp and has rendered its fat, add the onions and continue to cook until they are tender but not browned. Add the celery, stir, and cook for another minute. Pour in the reserved cup of cooking liquid from the quahogs and add the fish stock, potatoes, and herbs. Bring the mixture to a boil, then lower the heat to a simmer, cover, and cook for about 10 minutes or until the potatoes are tender but not mushy.

At this point the chowder base can be cooled and refrigerated until you are ready to finish it. To finish the chowder, add the scallops and cubed fish. Bring the mixture to a simmer, cover, and cook over medium-low heat for about 3 minutes. Chop the cooked quahogs and add them to the chowder along with the milk and butter. Season to taste with salt and pepper. Stir while the mixture becomes thoroughly heated; do not allow it to boil. When hot, ladle into soup bowls and serve immediately.

Wooden Boats and Iron Men

During the last half of the nineteenth century, Gloucester, Massachusetts, was home to the largest fleet of fishing schooners and earned the title of the leading fishing port in the world, in terms of landings. The fleet fished Georges Bank and the Grand Banks, engaging in dory fishing and seining. The schooners, beautiful and sleek, were referred to as "able handsome ladies" in their day and built to be fast. Their catches were legendary, but so was the loss of life for those who went to sea on them; between 1830 and 1897 alone nearly 700 vessels were lost and close to 4,000 men.

Shrimp and Scallop "Bisque"

Seared shrimp and scallops are the only solids in this creamy soup. Technically, it's not a bisque; the soup's base is thickened with pureed vegetables. The tomatoes and splash of cream lend a beautiful pink color. The base can be made a day ahead.

This recipe is a modification of one by Tracey Seaman, from a 1994 issue of *Food & Wine*.

Serves 6–8

2 tablespoons butter

4 carrots, chopped

4 stalks celery, chopped

2 onions, chopped

4 garlic cloves, minced

1 small fennel bulb, sliced (about ½ cup)

1 pound medium shrimp, peeled and deveined, with shells reserved

3 cups dry white wine

2 sprigs of thyme

3 sprigs of fresh parsley

3 cups water

2½ cups fish stock (homemade or commercially prepared)

16-ounce can plum tomatoes

1 teaspoon chopped fresh thyme

2 teaspoons chopped fresh parsley

½ cup light cream

Salt and pepper to taste

2 tablespoons olive oil

½ pound shucked scallops

Heat the butter in a large soup pot over medium heat. Add the carrot, celery, onion, garlic, and fennel and cook, stirring occasionally, for about 10 minutes, or until softened but not browned. Add the shrimp shells, wine, thyme and parsley sprigs.

Bring the mixture to a boil and cook for 2 minutes. Add the water, bring to a boil again, cover, lower the heat, and cook at a simmer for 20 minutes.

Remove the pot from the heat and with a slotted spoon transfer the vegetables to a food processor; puree. Once the vegetables have been removed from the stock, pour the stock through a fine-mesh strainer; discard the solids that remain in the strainer. Return the strained stock to the pot. Add the fish stock, tomatoes with their juices, and the pureed vegetable mixture. Bring to a boil; immediately lower the heat, cover, and cook at a low simmer for 30 minutes.

Add the chopped thyme and parsley, and the cream; season to taste with salt and pepper. At this point you can cool and refrigerate the soup for up to 24 hours, or until you are ready to finish it.

To finish, bring the soup to a gentle simmer over low heat. In a large skillet heat the olive oil over medium heat. When hot, add the scallops and cook, turning them with tongs, until they have a golden crust; remove to a platter. Add the shrimp to the skillet and cook until they are pink with golden edges. Remove from the heat.

Ladle the hot soup into warmed soup bowls and place a few shrimp and scallops in each. Serve immediately.

Linguiça, Littleneck Clam, and Mussel Soup

This soup is full of the rich, warm flavor of linguiça, a spicy Portuguese sausage. Littleneck clams and mussels are added to the soup pot and cooked in their shells after all the other ingredients have been incorporated, making this dish as handsome as it is flavorful. Be sure to have crusty bread on the table to dunk in the soup.

If you prefer, use all clams and eliminate the mussels.

Serves 4

1 tablespoon butter

1 tablespoon oil

1¹/₂ cups diced potatoes

Salt and pepper

¹/₂ cup chopped onion

¹/₄ pound linguiça, split lengthwise and cut in 1-inch pieces

2 garlic cloves, finely minced or pressed

1 red bell pepper, chopped

¹/₂ teaspoon chopped fresh thyme

¹/₂ teaspoon chopped fresh marjoram

1 tablespoon chopped fresh flat leaf parsley

1 teaspoon paprika

1 tablespoon Worcestershire sauce

¹/₂ cup red wine

3 cups fish stock (homemade or commercially prepared)

16 live littleneck clams, scrubbed clean

20 live mussels (shells about 2–2¹/₂ inches), scrubbed and de-bearded

In a Dutch oven or heavy soup pot heat the butter and oil over medium heat. Add the potatoes, sprinkle with a little salt and pepper, and cook, stirring occasionally, until lightly browned (about 3 minutes). Add the onion and continue cooking, stirring occasionally, until the onion is tender and translucent. Add the linguiça, garlic, and red pepper, and cook until the linguiça starts to curl and the pepper is tender. Add the herbs, paprika, Worcestershire sauce, and red wine. Continue cooking over medium heat, stirring occasionally, until the liquid is reduced by nearly half. Add the fish stock and bring the mixture to a boil. Add the clams, cover, lower the heat, and cook for 7 minutes. Add the mussels, cover, and cook for an additional 3 minutes, or until they open. (Use tongs to discard any clams and mussels that do not open.) Serve immediately.

To serve: Use tongs to place a few clams and mussels in each soup bowl (the shells will be open but still hinged together). Stir the soup and ladle it into the soup bowls.

Monkfish Stew

Not that many years ago monkfish was unknown to most Americans although popular in other countries. Fortunately, that has changed.

This soup is good any time of the year but the warm flavor of cayenne pepper makes it an especially good choice during cold weather. You can substitute any firm fleshed fish for a variation.

Serves 4

1 tablespoon olive oil

2 tablespoons butter

1⅓ cups chopped onions

1 cup chopped celery

1 garlic clove, finely minced or pressed

3 cups fresh baby spinach leaves

1 16-oz can crushed tomatoes with their juice

3½ cups fish stock (homemade or commercially prepared)

1 bay leaf

1 teaspoon chopped fresh thyme

¼ teaspoon cayenne pepper

1 pound monkfish, cut in 1-inch cubes

¼ cup chopped fresh flat leaf parsley

1 tablespoon chopped fresh tarragon

1 cup uncooked tubettini pasta (or other small shape)

Salt and pepper to taste

In a Dutch oven or heavy soup pot heat the oil and butter over medium heat. Add the onion, celery, and garlic, and cook, stirring occasionally, until the vegetables are tender and fragrant but not browned. Add the spinach and cook until wilted. Add the tomatoes, fish stock, bay leaf, thyme, and cayenne pepper; stir, and bring the mixture to a boil. When it reaches a boil, lower the heat, cover the pot, and simmer for 10 minutes. Add the fish chunks, parsley, tarragon, and pasta. Cover and continue to cook over medium-low heat for about 5 minutes, or until the fish and pasta are done. Season to taste with salt and pepper. Serve immediately.

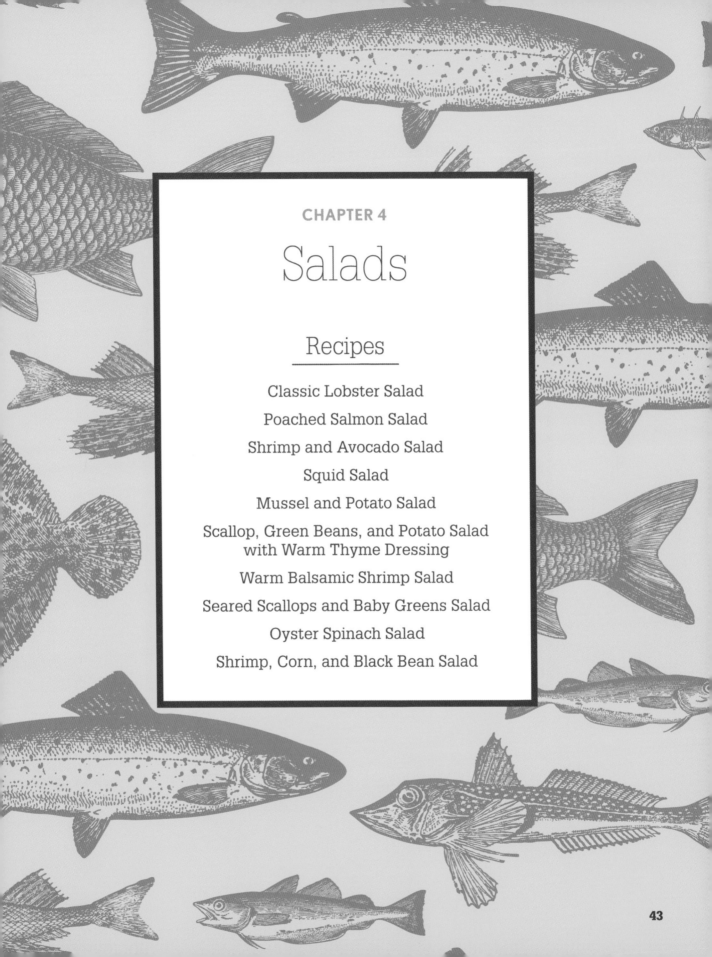

Salads

Recipes

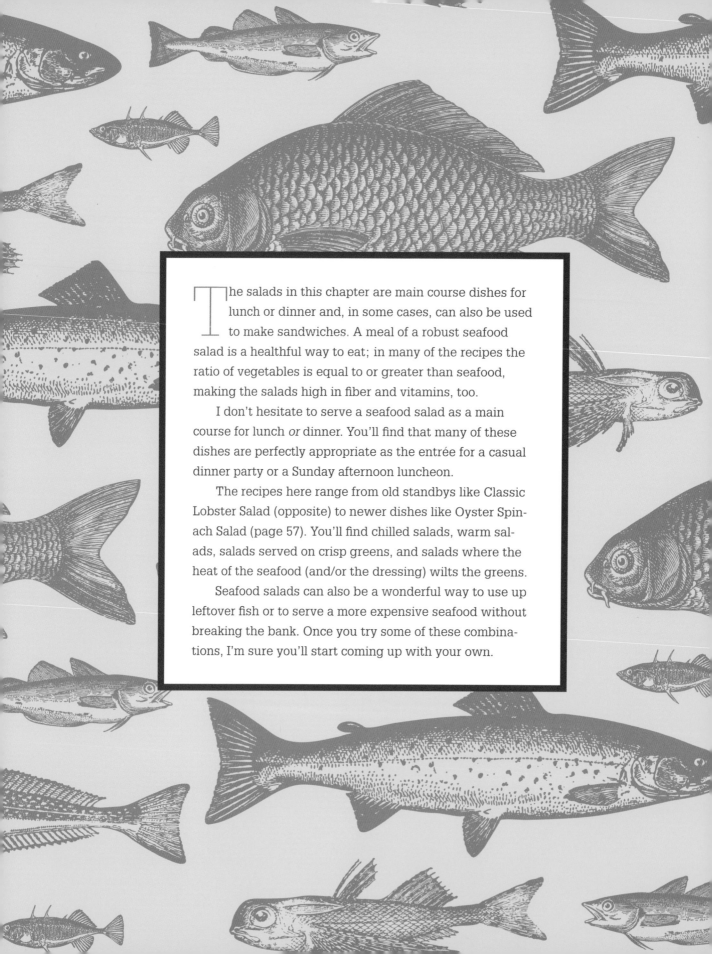

The salads in this chapter are main course dishes for lunch or dinner and, in some cases, can also be used to make sandwiches. A meal of a robust seafood salad is a healthful way to eat; in many of the recipes the ratio of vegetables is equal to or greater than seafood, making the salads high in fiber and vitamins, too.

I don't hesitate to serve a seafood salad as a main course for lunch *or* dinner. You'll find that many of these dishes are perfectly appropriate as the entrée for a casual dinner party or a Sunday afternoon luncheon.

The recipes here range from old standbys like Classic Lobster Salad (opposite) to newer dishes like Oyster Spinach Salad (page 57). You'll find chilled salads, warm salads, salads served on crisp greens, and salads where the heat of the seafood (and/or the dressing) wilts the greens.

Seafood salads can also be a wonderful way to use up leftover fish or to serve a more expensive seafood without breaking the bank. Once you try some of these combinations, I'm sure you'll start coming up with your own.

Classic Lobster Salad

There is nothing *new* about this recipe, but it's hard to improve on a classic. This is the way I learned to make lobster salad from my parents, with lobster left over from a summer lobster boil the night before. It works beautifully as a meal-in-one-dish salad or as the filling for a grilled lobster roll.

It's so easy to cook an extra lobster or two when you're having boiled lobsters for dinner. Try it, and enjoy homemade lobster salad the next day.

Serves 4

1 pound cooked lobster meat, coarsely chopped
(about 2 cups)

⅛ cup finely minced yellow or red onion

½ cup finely diced celery

2 tablespoons chopped fresh flat leaf parsley

½ cup mayonnaise

1 tablespoon fresh lemon juice

Salt and pepper to taste

1 head Boston lettuce or other tender-leaf lettuce

2 large tomatoes, cut into wedges

1 European cucumber, sliced

In a large bowl combine the lobster meat with the onion, celery, and parsley. Add the mayonnaise, lemon juice, and salt and pepper to taste, and toss to combine. Cover and refrigerate until ready to use.

To serve: Place a few leaves of Boston lettuce on each plate. Spoon a mound of lobster salad into the middle of the lettuce. Surround the lobster salad with tomato wedges and cucumber slices.

Fishermen don't choose fishing simply as a way to make a living. They choose it because they love being on the water and "messing about in boats" as much as any yachtsman.

Poached Salmon Salad

Cold poached salmon is one of life's simple pleasures. Here it makes a tasty salad with tender peas, spring potatoes, and lots of fresh dill—perfect for a spring weekend lunch, or light dinner. The salmon can be poached a day ahead.

Serves 4

1 pound salmon fillet

FOR THE POACHING LIQUID:

6 cups water

1 cup dry white wine

1 onion, quartered

1 carrot, sliced in 4 sections

1/4 teaspoon peppercorns

1 teaspoon salt

1 bay leaf

1/4 cup fresh parsley

FOR THE SALAD:

1 pound small fingerling potatoes (select equal-size potatoes)

1 box frozen peas, thawed but not cooked

1/2 cup chopped scallions

1/4 cup grated carrot

1 tablespoon chopped fresh parsley

2 tablespoons chopped fresh dill

1/2 cup mayonnaise

1 tablespoon fresh lemon juice

Salt and pepper to taste

1 head Bibb lettuce

1 lemon, cut in wedges

To poach the salmon: In a fish poaching pan with a rack, or in a roasting pan, combine the water, wine, onion, carrot, and seasonings. Place over high heat and bring to a boil. Lower heat and simmer for 20 minutes. Allow the liquid to cool before poaching the salmon.

Place the salmon on the rack in the poaching pan, or if you are using a roasting pan, place the salmon on a piece of heavy-duty foil to act as a rack before setting it in the poaching liquid. If the fish is not covered with liquid when it is set in the pan, add water until it is. Cover the pan and place over medium heat. Slowly bring to a boil (this should take about 15 minutes) and simmer for 1 minute. Turn off the heat and allow salmon to sit in the poaching liquid until it is cool enough to handle. Lift salmon out of poaching liquid and transfer to a platter; do not worry if the salmon breaks apart. Cover and refrigerate.

To make the salad: Place the whole potatoes in a steamer over boiling water and cook until tender, about 10–15 minutes. When cool enough to handle, halve and slice the potatoes. Transfer to a bowl and set aside to cool.

When the salmon and potatoes have cooled thoroughly, assemble the salad.

Remove and discard the skin from the poached salmon and flake the meat, removing any bones as you go; set aside.

In a large bowl combine the potatoes, peas, scallions, carrot, parsley, and dill. Add the mayonnaise and lemon juice, and toss to coat thoroughly. Add salt and pepper to taste.

To serve: Arrange a bed of lettuce leaves on each plate. Top with a spoonful of the potato/pea mixture. Place a portion of flaked salmon meat over each and serve with lemon wedges.

The Sounding Lead

In the days before the invention of electronic chromatoscopes, lorans, and depth finders that fishermen now use to figure out exactly where they are, what's on the bottom, and what kind of fish are in the water, they relied on some rather ingenious devices to find rich fishing grounds. One of these was the sounding lead. It was a narrow cylindrical item made of lead, about eight inches long and an inch in diameter. It was hollowed out at one end and had a line attached at the other, knotted at various intervals to determine depth. The hollow was filled with tallow, and when the lead was dropped overboard, it would dive nose first into the bottom. Whatever was on the bottom would become embedded in the tallow, and when the captain examined it—and more important, it is said, *smelled* it—he could tell the nature of the fishing grounds below them and whether to stay and fish, or move on.

Years ago, an old story goes, a couple of young crewmen on a Gloucester schooner devised a scheme to test the skills of their captain; before leaving port they secretly filled the tallow with some soil from town. When the time came to present the captain with the sounding lead, the two young crewmen held their breath and prepared for a good laugh as the captain examined it. He closed his eyes and took a long whiff. Then, looking at them with great seriousness, he said, "According to this, I reckon we're directly over Mrs. Murphy's garden."

"Next Sunday you'll be hirin' a boy to throw water on the windows to make ye go to sleep. . . . Do you know the best of gettin' ashore again?" "Hot bath?" said Harvey. His eyebrows were all white with dried spray. "That's good, but a night-shirt's better. I've been dreamim' o' night-shirts ever since we bent our mainsail. . . . It's home, Harve. It's home! Ye can sense it in the air. We're runnin' into the aidge of a hot wave naow, an' I can smell the bay-berries. Wonder if we'll get in fer supper."

—Rudyard Kipling, *Captains Courageous*

Shrimp and Avocado Salad

This dish makes a beautiful presentation for a special lunch with friends. Half of an avocado is piled to overflowing with shrimp salad, and the other half is sliced and fanned out decoratively beside it. If you do not know how to tell if an avocado is ripe, ask for help at your market.

I developed this salad as a way to use Maine shrimp, but they are not always available. If you can get them, great; otherwise, use the smallest Atlantic or Gulf shrimp. If the smallest shrimp you can get is "medium," cut them into thirds.

Serves 4

1 pound cleaned and cooked shrimp
  (see page 106), cooled

½ cup finely diced carrot

½ cup julienned celery root (celeriac)

¼ cup mayonnaise

4 teaspoons fresh lemon juice

2 teaspoons finely chopped fresh parsley

Salt and pepper to taste

4 perfectly ripe avocados

1 lemon, cut into 8 wedges

In a large bowl toss the shrimp with the carrot and celery root. In a separate bowl whisk together the mayonnaise, lemon juice, parsley, and salt and pepper to taste. Pour the dressing over the shrimp mixture and toss gently to coat evenly. Cover and refrigerate until ready to use.

To serve: Halve the avocados, and remove and discard the pit. Place half of an avocado on each plate; skin the other half, slice it into ¼-inch sections, and fan out on the plate next to the avocado still in its skin. Divide the shrimp salad into four portions and spoon into the avocado halves. The salad will be more than the avocado can hold, so let it fall onto the plate next to the fanned slices. Put two lemon wedges on each plate.

Squid Salad

Squid has a delicate flavor that can be lost in deep frying and overpowered in tomato sauce dishes. Here sautéed squid is presented barely adorned. Tossed with a few fresh vegetables and a tangy balsamic vinaigrette, the squid takes center stage.

Serves 4-6

1½ cups cleaned and trimmed fresh broccoli rabe

1 tablespoon olive oil

1½–2 pounds cleaned squid, cut in ¼-inch rings,
    tentacles separated and cut in half (see page 177)

1 garlic clove, finely minced

1 tablespoon fresh lemon juice

Freshly ground black pepper

½ cup thinly sliced red onion

½ cup julienned roasted red bell pepper
    (1 large pepper; see page 5)

⅓ cup pitted and halved Kalamata olives

¼ cup loosely packed and chopped flat leaf parsley

FOR THE VINAIGRETTE:

3 sun-dried tomatoes

1½ tablespoons balsamic vinegar

1½ tablespoons red wine vinegar

1 garlic clove, finely minced or pressed

½ teaspoon salt

⅓ cup olive oil

1 tablespoon chopped fresh basil

3 cups mixed greens, including some arugula,
    if available

Bring a large pot of lightly salted water to a boil. Add the broccoli rabe and cook at a boil for 3 minutes. Drain in a colander and plunge into a large pan of cold water to stop the cooking; set aside to drain.

Heat the oil in a large heavy skillet over medium heat. When hot but not smoking, add the squid rings and tentacles, and cook until the squid is opaque white with some golden edges. Transfer the squid to a plate to cool.

Chop the broccoli rabe into 1-inch pieces. Add it, with the garlic, to the same skillet used for the squid and cook over medium heat for about 2 minutes, turning occasionally with a spatula. Remove from the heat and add the lemon juice and some freshly ground black pepper; set aside to cool.

In a large bowl combine the cooled squid and broccoli rabe with the onion, pepper, olives, and parsley. Toss.

To make the vinaigrette: Place the tomatoes in a glass bowl and add boiling water to barely cover them. Let sit 15 minutes. Drain off the liquid and chop the tomatoes very fine.

In a small bowl whisk together the rest of the ingredients. Add the tomatoes and stir. Pour over the squid salad and toss.

To serve: place some of the mixed greens on each plate. Toss the salad again before spooning a portion on each plate of greens. Serve with bread and wedges of ripe tomato.

*Note: This salad should be served slightly warm, or at room temperature. If you are going to make it in advance, cover the salad and refrigerate it. Bring to room temperature before serving.

Mussel and Potato Salad

Potato salads are one of the great traditions of summer. Here, steamed mussels are added, and the whole is blended with a tangy dressing. On a bed of greens and surrounded with fresh summer vegetables, this dish makes a tasty meal or a great addition to a picnic spread.

Serves 6–8

5 pounds live mussels, scrubbed, de-bearded, and cooked (see page 106), with ½ cup of cooking liquid strained and reserved

7 tablespoons olive oil

3 pounds small red-skinned potatoes, steamed until tender

2 scallions, chopped

1 cup chopped celery

1 tablespoon minced shallot

1 garlic clove, finely minced

1 tablespoon chopped fresh flat leaf parsley

2 tablespoons white wine vinegar

1 tablespoon fresh lemon juice

1 tablespoon Dijon mustard

1 teaspoon anchovy paste

3 tablespoons sour cream

Pick the cooked mussel meat from the shells, removing any grit or beards that you may have missed, and set aside.

Combine the reserved ½ cup of mussel broth with 3 tablespoons of oil. Pour over the mussels, toss gently, and set aside.

Dice the potatoes and place them in a large bowl. Add the mussels, scallions, and celery. Toss gently.

In a separate bowl combine the shallot, garlic, parsley, remaining 4 tablespoons of olive oil, vinegar, lemon juice, mustard, anchovy paste, and sour cream. Blend well.

Pour the dressing over the potato/mussel mixture and toss gently to coat evenly. Cover and refrigerate for at least 1 hour to allow the flavors to develop.

Allow to sit at room temperature for 10 minutes before serving. Serve on a bed of lettuce, with wedges of tomato and cucumber.

Scallop, Green Bean, and Potato Salad with Warm Thyme Dressing

A warm thyme-flavored dressing is a delicious complement to this salad. The hearty flavors are perfect for fall, the time of year when bay scallops are harvested and backyard gardens are still producing late-season green beans and tomatoes.

Serves 4–6

3 tablespoons butter

1 pound shucked scallops

¼ cup minced shallots

1¼ cups dry white wine

1¼ cups light cream

2 tablespoons finely chopped fresh thyme

Salt and pepper to taste

1 tablespoon olive oil

3 cups peeled and diced potatoes, boiled until just tender

1 pound green beans, blanched and cut into 1-inch pieces

1½ cups diced tomatoes (about 2 large beefsteak tomatoes)

1 head butter or Boston lettuce, washed and dried

Heat 2 tablespoons of butter in a large, lightly oiled skillet. Add the scallops and cook in a single layer over medium heat, turning with tongs, until golden on all sides. Transfer to an ovenproof dish, cover loosely with foil, and place in a warm oven or warming drawer.

Add the remaining tablespoon of butter to the skillet. Add the shallots and cook over medium heat until they are tender but not browned. Add the wine, raise the heat and bring to a boil, scraping the bottom of the pan with a wooden spoon to loosen any bits of scallop or shallot adhering to the bottom. Lower the heat and add the cream and thyme. Bring the mixture to a low simmer and continue to cook gently, stirring, until reduced

by about one-third. Add salt and pepper to taste. Remove from heat and cover.

Heat the olive oil in a large skillet. Add the potatoes and toss until evenly coated. Continue cooking the potatoes over medium heat until they start to take on a pale golden color. Add the green beans and continue cooking, turning with a spatula, until the potatoes are a deep golden color with a slight crispness to the edges and the green beans are hot. Remove from the heat and transfer immediately to a large bowl. Add the scallops, with any juices that have formed in the dish, and toss gently with a large spoon. Pour the thyme sauce over the mixture. Toss gently again, coating evenly. Add the diced tomatoes and toss until evenly distributed.

Arrange the lettuce on individual plates. Top each with a portion of the warm scallop salad. Serve immediately.

Scallops

Whether you buy scallops shucked or in the shell, always remove the little crescent-shaped piece of gristle that adheres to the scallop meat itself. At first it will be hard to notice, but once you know how to recognize it, it's easy to spot. It's perfectly edible but becomes rubbery when cooked. I set them aside as a treat for my dog.

Warm Balsamic Shrimp Salad

In this "wilted" salad, grilled shrimp top a bed of greens mixed with sliced avocado and tomato, and the whole thing is topped with a warm dressing of balsamic vinegar and caramelized red onion slices. It's a pretty meal-in-one-dish that is made right before serving so be sure to have all your ingredients prepped and measured before you start.

A pound of jumbo shrimp is usually ten to twelve shrimp. Plan on serving five shrimp per person if you will be serving this dish as the main course; when you go to the fish market, buy the shrimp by count, not weight.

Serves 2

3 cups mixed baby salad greens

1½ tablespoons fresh lemon juice

3 tablespoons balsamic vinegar

1 tablespoon, plus 1 teaspoon, sugar

6 tablespoons olive oil

½ large red onion, very thinly sliced

1 garlic clove, coarsely chopped

10 jumbo shrimp, peeled and deveined (save and freeze the shrimp shells for stock)

1 tablespoon finely chopped fresh basil

2 tablespoons grated Parmesan cheese

Freshly ground black pepper to taste

½ cup Garlic Croutons (page 169)

1 ripe avocado, peeled and sliced

1 large ripe tomato or 2 small ones, washed and quartered

Arrange the cleaned greens on two large dinner plates and cover with a barely damp paper towel.

Combine the lemon juice, vinegar, and sugar in a glass measuring cup; stir and set aside.

Heat 3 tablespoons of olive oil in a skillet over medium heat. Add the onion slices and cook until soft but not browned. Remove onions with a slotted spoon and set aside Add the garlic and shrimp to the hot skillet and sauté until the shrimp are pink and have golden edges, approximately 2–3 minutes. Remove the shrimp, place on a platter, and cover loosely with a foil tent. Let rest while you complete the dish (this will take about 5 minutes).

Scoop the cooked garlic out of the pan and discard. Add the remaining 3 tablespoons of oil and heat until warm. Return the onion slices to the pan and turn off the heat. Pour in the vinegar mixture and stir.

Assemble the salad: Remove the paper towel from the greens. Sprinkle the basil, Parmesan cheese, pepper, and croutons over the lettuce. Arrange the sliced avocado and tomato wedges around the edges of the plates. Place the warm shrimp over the salad, including any juices that have formed on the platter, and top with the warm dressing and onions from the pan. Serve immediately.

Seared Scallops and Baby Greens Salad

This salad is the heart of simplicity, and special enough for a casual dinner or Sunday lunch with friends. Make it in the summer, when corn and tomatoes are at their peak

Prepare the vinaigrette first and have the greens ready so that the salad can be served as soon as the scallops are seared.

Serves 4

FOR THE VINAIGRETTE:

2 tablespoons fresh lemon juice

½ teaspoon Dijon mustard

½ teaspoon sugar or honey

⅓ cup olive oil

1½ teaspoons chopped fresh flat leaf parsley

1½ teaspoons chopped fresh chives

1½ teaspoons chopped fresh basil

Salt and pepper to taste

FOR THE SALAD:

4 cups mixed baby salad greens

1 cup fresh corn kernels

½ cup grated carrot

12 cherry tomatoes, halved

1 tablespoon olive oil

1 pound shucked scallops

To make the vinaigrette, whisk together all ingredients in a bowl. Set aside.

Toss the mixed baby greens in a bowl with the corn, carrot, and cherry tomatoes. Set aside.

Place the oil in a large, heavy skillet over medium heat. When hot but not smoking, add the scallops and cook, turning with tongs, until they have a golden crust. As they are done, transfer to a platter.

Divide the tossed greens among four plates. Top with the warm, seared scallops and pour a little dressing over each. Serve immediately.

Oyster Spinach Salad

This is a beautiful meal-in-one-dish salad for fall: oysters are at their peak, as are spinach, apples, and walnuts, and the flavors are perfect complements for one another. The vivid colors—deep green spinach and golden yellow cornmeal-crusted oysters—make a stunning presentation. This is one of those salads where the warm dressing "wilts" the greens. Serve with warm cornbread.

Serves 4

1 pound shucked oysters

1/2 cup yellow cornmeal

6 slices lean bacon

1 large red onion, halved and thinly sliced

1 cooking apple, peeled and grated

1 tablespoon sugar

1/4 cup cider vinegar

1/4 cup dry white wine

1/4 teaspoon dry mustard

Salt and pepper to taste

2 tablespoons butter

1 10-ounce bag fresh baby spinach, cleaned

1/2 cup grated Asiago cheese

1/2 cup coarsely chopped walnuts, toasted

1 tablespoon finely chopped fresh flat leaf parsley

1 cup Garlic Croutons (page 169)

Dredge the oysters in the cornmeal and set aside.

Cook the bacon in a large skillet until crisp. Remove the bacon from the pan and transfer it to brown paper or a paper towel to drain. Add the onion to the hot bacon fat and cook over medium heat just until wilted—do not let the onion brown or become crisp. Add the grated apple and continue cooking until it becomes completely soft, about 1 minute. Add the sugar, vinegar, wine, dry mustard, salt, and pepper. Stir well and continue cooking for about 1 minute, or until the sugar is dissolved. Turn off the heat.

In another large skillet melt the butter over medium-high heat. Add the oysters, without crowding the pan, and cook until golden on both sides. This will take about 2 minutes per side. As they are done, transfer to an ovenproof plate and place in a warm oven or warming drawer.

To assemble the salad: Place the spinach in a large salad bowl. Crumble the bacon and add to the spinach along with the cheese, walnuts, and parsley. Toss to combine. Pour the warm onion/apple/vinegar mixture over the spinach and toss. Add the croutons, toss again, and divide among the four serving plates. Place an equal portion of cooked oysters on each serving of spinach salad. Serve immediately.

Shrimp, Corn, and Black Bean Salad

Jumbo shrimp with a crisp cornmeal coating atop a meal-in-one-dish salad of black beans, fresh corn, crisp red pepper, and scallions yield a fabulous combination of summer flavors and colors. The inspiration came from a meal I had at El Mirador Restaurant in San Antonio, Texas. A cilantro dressing finishes the dish.

Four jumbo shrimp per person is just right if you're serving this for lunch; for dinner, you may want to increase that to five.

Serves 6

FOR THE VEGETABLE SALAD:

2¹/₂ cups fresh corn kernels

2 cups cooked black beans, drained and completely cooled (rinsed if canned)

¹/₄ cup chopped scallion

¹/₂ cup chopped red bell pepper

¹/₂ cup loosely packed chopped fresh cilantro

1 teaspoon salt

¹/₂ teaspoon freshly ground black pepper

FOR THE SHRIMP:

24 jumbo shrimp

¹/₄ cup buttermilk

1 egg, beaten

1 cup yellow cornmeal

Pinch of salt and pepper

2 tablespoons olive oil

2 tablespoons butter

¹/₂ cup Cilantro Dressing (see page 165)

1 head Romaine lettuce

To make the salad: Combine the corn, beans, scallion, red pepper, cilantro, salt, and pepper in a large bowl. Toss well, cover, and refrigerate.

To prepare the shrimp: Shell and devein the shrimp, leaving the tails intact. (Save and freeze the shrimp shells for stock.) Place the buttermilk in a small bowl; place the egg in a second bowl; and place the cornmeal with the salt and pepper in a third bowl.

In a large cast-iron skillet heat 1 tablespoon of oil and 1 tablespoon of butter over medium heat.

Dip each shrimp in buttermilk, then cornmeal, then beaten egg, and then in the cornmeal again. Press the shrimp into the cornmeal each time so that a good layer adheres to it. Place 12 of the shrimp in the hot pan, being careful not to crowd them, and cook until golden on each side, about 1–2 minutes per side. Turn with tongs only once during the cooking process. As the shrimp are cooked, remove them to a plate lined with brown paper or paper towel. Repeat this process with the remaining oil and butter for the last 12 shrimp.

To assemble the salad: Pour the cilantro dressing over the corn and black bean mixture and toss, thoroughly coating them. Place an equal portion of salad greens on each dinner plate. Top with a mound of the corn and black bean mixture. Arrange 4 shrimp over the top. Serve immediately.

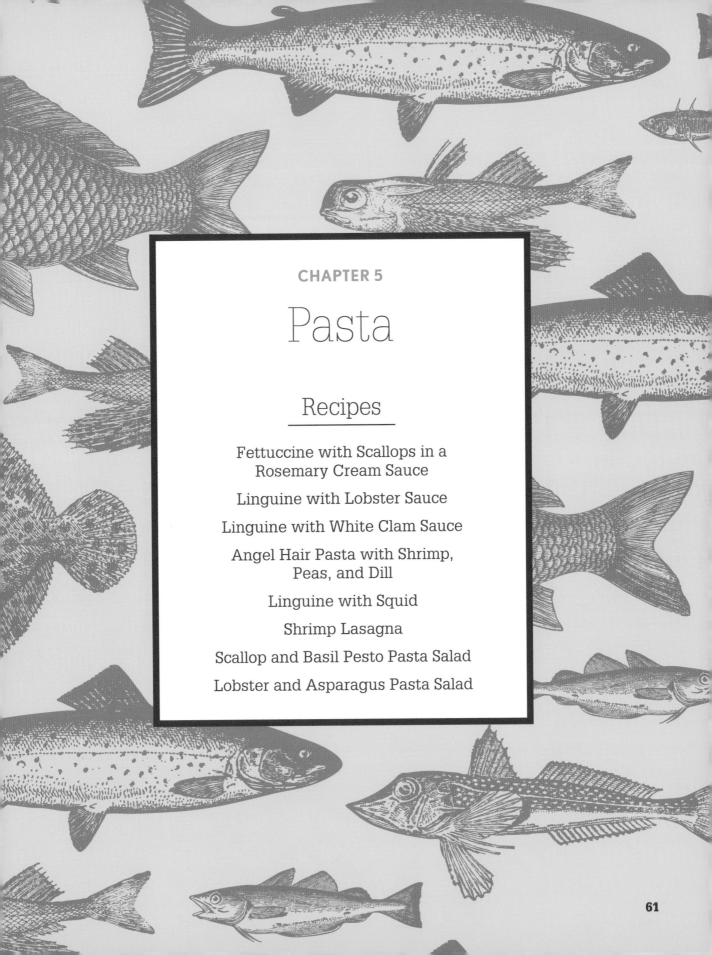

Pasta

Recipes

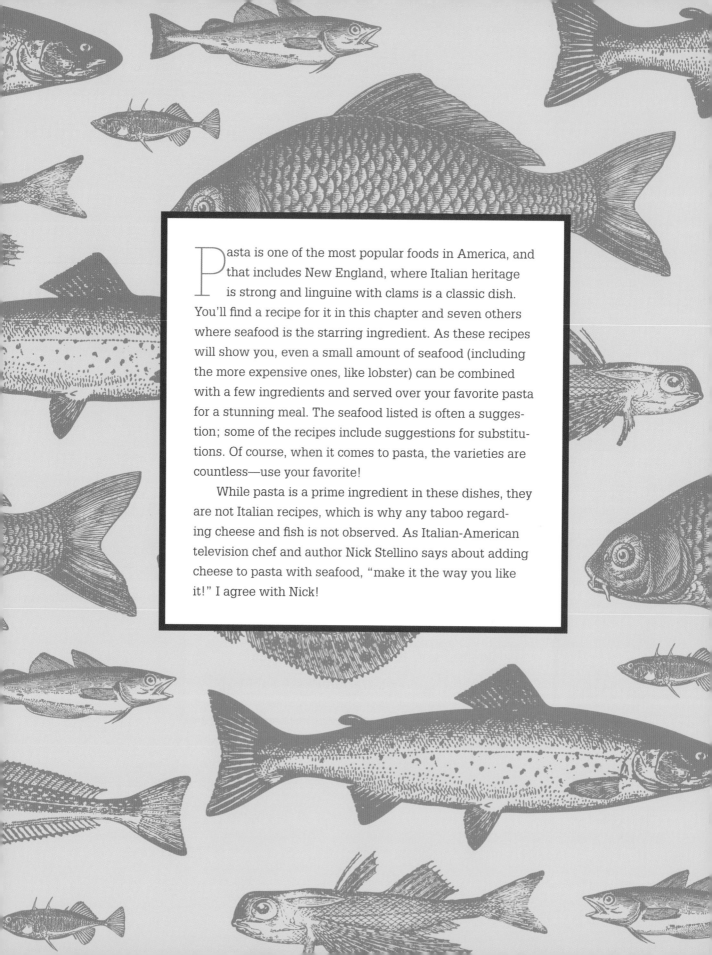

Pasta is one of the most popular foods in America, and that includes New England, where Italian heritage is strong and linguine with clams is a classic dish. You'll find a recipe for it in this chapter and seven others where seafood is the starring ingredient. As these recipes will show you, even a small amount of seafood (including the more expensive ones, like lobster) can be combined with a few ingredients and served over your favorite pasta for a stunning meal. The seafood listed is often a suggestion; some of the recipes include suggestions for substitutions. Of course, when it comes to pasta, the varieties are countless—use your favorite!

While pasta is a prime ingredient in these dishes, they are not Italian recipes, which is why any taboo regarding cheese and fish is not observed. As Italian-American television chef and author Nick Stellino says about adding cheese to pasta with seafood, "make it the way you like it!" I agree with Nick!

Fettuccine with Scallops in a Rosemary Cream Sauce

A golden brown, rosemary-flavored cream sauce gives this dish a flavor well suited for fall and winter. Once you have the ingredients at hand, the sauce can be assembled in the time it takes to cook the pasta. Monkfish or cod can be used in place of the scallops.

This is very good served with Stewed Swiss Chard (page 130).

Serves 4

3 tablespoons butter

1 pound shucked scallops (or cubed monkfish or cod)

3 tablespoons finely minced shallots

2 garlic cloves, finely minced

1 cup dry white wine

1 pound tomato fettuccine (or plain fettuccine)

1 teaspoon finely chopped fresh rosemary

1 cup light cream

2 tablespoons grated Parmesan cheese

Salt and pepper to taste

1 tablespoon finely chopped fresh flat leaf parsley

Melt 2 tablespoons of butter in a large skillet over medium heat. Add the scallops and cook, turning them carefully with tongs, until they are golden on all sides. As the scallops are cooked, transfer them to a plate, and cover with a loose foil tent. When all the scallops have been cooked, add the shallots and garlic to the pan and cook over medium heat until tender and fragrant. Add the wine, stirring to scrape the garlic and shallots from the bottom of the pan. Cook until the wine is reduced by half.

While the wine is reducing, bring a large pot of lightly salted cold water to a boil. When the sauce is nearly complete, cook the pasta.

Add the rosemary to the reduced wine sauce, stirring quickly, and then pour in the cream. Lower the heat slightly, then whisk in the remaining tablespoon of butter and the Parmesan cheese. Pour in the liquid that has formed on the plate with the scallops, stir, and season with salt and pepper to taste. Add the scallops and turn the heat to the lowest setting; keep the skillet partially covered.

Place the cooked and drained fettuccine in a large pasta serving bowl. Spoon the scallops and sauce over all, sprinkle with parsley, toss, and serve.

During the 1980s, New Bedford was the nation's most profitable fishing port. This status was due not only to the size of the fleet and catches but also because of the large quantities of scallops and yellowtail flounder in the total landings, both of which commanded high prices.

Linguine with Lobster Sauce

This recipe is a delicious way to use lobster meat left over from a boiled lobster dinner. It's a quick dish to make; add a green salad and crusty loaf of bread and you have a memorable meal.

You can substitute lump crabmeat or cubed monkfish for the lobster.

Serves 4

2 tablespoons olive oil

1 tablespoon butter

2 garlic cloves, finely minced

2 tablespoons minced shallots

2 cups coarsely chopped cooked lobster meat
(about 1 pound; or lump crabmeat,
or cubed monkfish)

4 tablespoons cognac

2 cups peeled and chopped plum tomatoes

1 cup dry white wine

2 teaspoons finely chopped fresh tarragon or basil

Salt and pepper to taste

1 pound linguine, cooked al dente

4 tablespoons grated Parmesan cheese

Heat the olive oil and butter in a large skillet. Add the garlic and shallots, and cook over medium heat until tender and translucent but not browned. Add the lobster meat and continue to cook for another 2 minutes. Pour in the cognac and light with a match. When the flame dies, add the tomatoes, wine, and herbs. Bring to a simmer, stir, cover partially, and cook over low heat for 5 minutes. Add salt and pepper to taste.

Toss the cooked and drained pasta with the Parmesan cheese. Put a serving of pasta on individual plates and top with lobster sauce. Serve immediately.

> **Variation:** For a creamy sauce, add ½ cup of light cream to the mixture after the tomatoes, wine, and herbs have simmered for 5 minutes. Continue to heat until the mixture returns to a simmer, and add salt and pepper to taste.

Linguine with White Clam Sauce

Buy fresh littleneck clams or fresh small quahogs if you have the time to steam them and pick the meat; otherwise, buy canned baby clams and bottled clam juice. There are as many "authentic" versions of this recipe are there are varieties of pasta. This is my husband's recipe and everyone loves it!

This sauce can be made ahead, refrigerated and served the next day.

Serves 4-6

1½ cups clam meat; if using fresh clams in the shell, about 18 small quahogs or 24 littlenecks will produce this yield

¼ cup olive oil

2 tablespoons butter

¾ cup minced celery

¾ cup minced onion

3 garlic cloves, finely minced or pressed

1 tablespoon unbleached flour

1 tablespoon light cream

½ cup dry white wine

1 cup clam broth (from steaming the clams, or bottled)

⅓ cup finely chopped fresh flat leaf parsley

1½ pounds linguine, cooked al dente

½ cup grated Parmesan cheese for topping

To cook the clams: If you are using fresh clams in the shell follow the directions on page 106 and reserve 1 cup of the broth, strained, for this recipe.

To make the sauce: Heat the olive oil and butter in a large, heavy skillet over medium heat until the butter is sizzling hot. Add the celery, onion, and garlic, and cook, stirring occasionally, until tender but not browned. Sprinkle in the flour and stir until it is incorporated. Add the cream, stirring until it is blended and the cream and flour are thick. Add the wine, stir, and cook until the wine is blended with the cream sauce. Add the clam broth and stir. Lower the heat and allow to barely simmer, partially covered, for 5–10 minutes.

Add the clams and parsley to the sauce. Stir, cover, and keep over the lowest heat while you drain the pasta.

Place a portion of pasta on each dinner plate and top with a generous amount of clam sauce. Top with a little grated Parmesan cheese, if desired. Serve immediately.

Angel Hair Pasta with Shrimp, Peas, and Dill

I developed this recipe for Maine shrimp, which are available fresh only a few months of the year but small or medium Atlantic or Gulf shrimp work well, too.

Serves 4

3 tablespoons butter

½ cup finely diced onion

½ cup finely diced carrot

2 tablespoons flour

2¼ cups milk

¼ cup dry white wine

2 tablespoons chopped fresh flat leaf parsley

2 teaspoons chopped fresh dill

1½ pounds shrimp, uncooked, shelled and cleaned

1½ cups peas (fresh or frozen but not cooked)

1 pound angel hair pasta

Salt and pepper to taste

In a large, heavy skillet melt the butter over medium heat. Cook the onion and carrot until tender. Sprinkle in the flour and stir until it is incorporated. Add the milk slowly, stirring constantly and allowing the sauce to thicken after each addition, until all the milk is added and the sauce is thick. Add the wine and continue cooking to allow the sauce to thicken again. Add the herbs, shrimp, peas, salt and pepper. Stir gently and keep on the lowest heat for about 10 minutes.

In the meantime, add the angel hair pasta to a pot of boiling water. When the pasta is cooked al dente, drain and transfer it to a wide, shallow bowl. Top with the shrimp sauce, toss, and serve immediately.

Seafood Is Not Free for the Taking

Visiting a New England fishing port on a clear day at the beginning of summer can be a real treat. The warmth of the sun, the sound of the water lapping against the sides of the boats, and fresh salt air soothe the soul and whet the appetite.

At the end of the day when the lobster boats come in, you're likely to find the fishermen selling some of their catch at the dock. It doesn't get any fresher than this, and the price is a bargain, too.

But if you decide to haggle over price, remember that for the fisherman, lobsters are not free. Lobstermen make enormous investments to go fishing. Today in New England it is not unusual for a lobsterman with a "day boat" to have a sizable boat mortgage ($50,000 to $100,000 is not uncommon), and gear in the water—traps, line, buoys—that is worth more than $60,000. Then there are the expenses of boat and crew insurance, dockage, fuel, and the crew's wages to pay before the lobsterman sees a dime.

Linguine with Squid

This sauce is flavored with sun-dried tomatoes, sweet red peppers, and a little Madeira wine, all pulled together with a splash of light cream or fish stock. The squid is lightly sautéed before it becomes part of the sauce, giving it more flavor and a tender texture.

Serves 4

1 cup sun-dried tomatoes

3 tablespoons olive oil

1½ pounds cleaned squid (see page 177), cut in ¼" rings, with chopped tentacles if purchased whole

¾ cup julienned red bell pepper

½ cup thinly sliced onion

4 garlic cloves, minced

½ cup light cream (or fish stock)

4 tablespoons chopped fresh flat leaf parsley

4 tablespoons chopped fresh basil

2 tablespoons Madeira wine

1 pound linguine, cooked al dente

Cut the sun-dried tomatoes into quarters and put in a bowl. Add enough boiling water to barely cover them and let sit for 15 minutes. Drain, reserving ¼ cup of the liquid for the sauce. Set aside.

In the meantime, add the lingune pasta to a pot of boiling water. When the pasta is cooked al dente, drain and transfer it to a wide, shallow bowl.

Place the oil in a large, heavy skillet over medium heat. When hot but not smoking, add the squid. Cook, stirring, for about 1 minute, or until the squid begins to turn opaque white. Add the red pepper, onion, garlic, and sun-dried tomatoes, and continue cooking over medium heat until the vegetables are tender but not browned, about 2 minutes. Add the cream (or fish stock), herbs, wine, and ¼ cup of reserved liquid from the sun-dried tomatoes. Stir and continue cooking until the sauce is thoroughly heated.

Pour the sauce over the hot pasta, toss, and serve.

Shrimp Lasagna

Seven delicate layers of noodles sandwich a filling of spinach, cheeses, a little tomato sauce, and lots of fresh shrimp. For a variation, substitute crabmeat or thin fillets of flounder or fluke for the shrimp. This dish freezes well, so consider making two and popping one in the freezer for an effortless but spectacular meal later.

Serves 6 (makes one 8-inch-square lasagna)

1 box frozen spinach, thawed and well drained

2 eggs, beaten

2 garlic cloves, crushed

1 pound ricotta cheese

¼ cup grated Parmesan cheese

¼ cup packed fresh basil leaves

½ cup grated mozzarella cheese

¼ cup goat cheese

2 cups marinara sauce

Lasagna noodles* (7 sheets of Ondine® or sufficient pasta to make 7 thin layers)

1 pound medium shrimp, uncooked, shelled and deveined (or variation; see headnote)

The Best Commercial Lasagna

If you are not going to make your own lasagna noodles, use the thin, delicate noodles that do *not* need to be cooked before assembling the lasagna. Ondine is my favorite brand and the closest thing to fresh-from-scratch I've found. Each package includes two 8 inch-square baking pans and enough noodles for two generous lasagnas.

Preheat oven to 350°F.

Place the spinach, eggs, garlic, ricotta and Parmesan cheeses, basil, ¼ cup of mozzarella, and goat cheese in a food processor fitted with the metal blade. Pulse until ingredients are well combined. Transfer to a large bowl and stir in 1½ cups of marinara sauce.

Pour ¼ cup of the remaining marinara sauce in the bottom of an 8x8-inch lasagna pan. Cover with a layer of lasagna noodles. Spread ⅔ cup of the spinach/cheese mixture on the noodles. Lay ⅙ of the cleaned shrimp over the spinach/cheese mixture and top with a sheet of lasagna noodles. Repeat this process until you have used up all the noodles and all the filling and shrimp, ending with a layer of lasagna noodles. Pour the remaining ¼ cup of marinara sauce over the top and sprinkle with the remaining ¼ cup of mozzarella cheese. Cover the pan with foil and bake for 30 minutes. Remove the foil and bake for 15–20 minutes more.

Place the pan on a cooling rack and let sit, covered with a *loose* foil tent, for 15 minutes. Cut into squares and serve.

Note: Ondine lasagna noodles are very thinly rolled. If you are using a thicker noodle, you will probably want to reduce this recipe to 5 layers of noodles and adjust each layer of the filling accordingly.

Scallop and Pesto Pasta Salad

This meal-in-one-dish is a good summer recipe, especially if you have a vegetable garden and an overabundance of basil. You can substitute shrimp, grilled tuna, swordfish, monkfish, cod, haddock, or pollack for the scallops.

This salad can be made in advance, which allows the flavors to develop and makes serving dinner even easier for you!

Serves 6

1 large eggplant, unpeeled and diced (about 8 cups)

3 tablespoons olive oil

¼ teaspoon salt

3 sweet red bell peppers, roasted (see page 5)

1 pound shucked scallops

1 tablespoon butter

1 pound small pasta shells

1 cup Basic Basil Pesto (see page 168)

¼ cup mayonnaise

2½ cups diced plum tomatoes

3 tablespoons chopped fresh flat leaf parsley

Preheat oven to 400°F.

Place the eggplant in a large shallow pan and sprinkle with 2 tablespoons of olive oil and the salt. Toss to coat evenly. Bake for approximately 35 minutes, turning with a spatula once or twice during baking. The eggplant should not be mushy. Cool on a rack.

Cut the peppers into thin slices, about ¼ inch by 1 inch. Set aside on a plate.

Heat the remaining tablespoon of olive oil and the butter in a large skillet over medium heat. Place the scallops in the skillet and sear them, turning them with tongs as they cook, until they are golden on all sides. When completely cooked, remove to a plate along with any juices that have formed in the pan and set aside.

Bring a large pot of lightly salted water to a boil and cook the pasta. While it is cooking, prepare the pesto and combine it with the mayonnaise in a small bowl. When the pasta is cooked, drain it and transfer it to a large bowl. Spoon the pesto mixture over the pasta while it is still warm and toss well. Set aside to cool to room temperature.

Add the roasted eggplant, red peppers, scallops (or substitution), tomatoes, and parsley to the pasta, including any juices that have formed on the plate with the scallops and peppers. Toss gently. Cover and let sit for 5 minutes. Serve at room temperature.

Lobster and Asparagus Pasta Salad

Lobster meat, asparagus spears, and small pasta shells—blended with a classic vinaigrette—make a pretty and flavorful salad. This meal-in-one-dish is as appropriate for dinner as it is for a special picnic. You can substitute monkfish or lump crabmeat for the lobster. Make this when local asparagus is in season.

Serves 4-6

FOR THE SALAD:

1 pound cooked lobster meat, coarsely chopped

12 grape tomatoes, quartered

1 pound tender asparagus, blanched and
    cut in 1-inch pieces

2 cups small pasta shells, cooked al dente

1 head Boston lettuce

FOR THE VINAIGRETTE:

$1/3$ cup olive oil

1 teaspoon Dijon mustard

1 teaspoon honey

2 tablespoons white wine vinegar

1 tablespoon fresh lemon juice

$1/2$ teaspoon chopped fresh tarragon

1 teaspoon chopped fresh flat leaf parsley

1 teaspoon chopped fresh chives

Salt and pepper to taste

In a large bowl combine all the salad ingredients except the lettuce. Toss gently.

In a separate bowl whisk together the vinaigrette ingredients. Pour over the salad and toss. Allow to sit for 10 minutes.

Arrange some lettuce on each plate. Toss the salad again and spoon a portion onto each lettuce bed. Serve immediately.

CHAPTER 6

Main Course Dishes

Recipes

Basic Baked Fish Fillets
or Steaks

Basic Sautéed Fish Fillets
or Steaks

Basic Grilled Fish Steaks

Pan-Seared Sea Trout with
Tomatoes and Herbs

Pan-fried Flounder with
Lemon and Wine Sauce

Crispy Herbed Tautog with
Honey Mustard Butter

Old-Fashioned Fish and Chips

Pan-fried Crispy
Mackerel Fillets

Fish Cakes

Cod Provençale

Stuffed Squid

Curried Monkfish

Stuffed Fluke

Broiled Bluefish with
Anchovy Vinaigrette

Broiled Fish with
Red Pepper Pesto

Broiled Mackerel with
Mustard Butter

Fish Baked with Basil Pesto

Roasted Whole Sea Bass

Monkfish Kebabs

Soy and Ginger Grilled Tuna

Seafood Tacos

Basic Boiled or
Steamed Shellfish

Basic Sautéed Shellfish

Basic Grilled or Broiled
Shellfish Kebabs

Basic Grilled or Broiled
Shellfish in the Shell

Mussels Steamed in
Wine and Herbs

Spicy Cajun Shrimp

Crab Cakes

Oyster Bread Pudding

Crab Soufflé

Lobster Pie

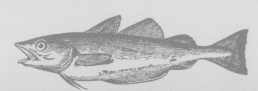

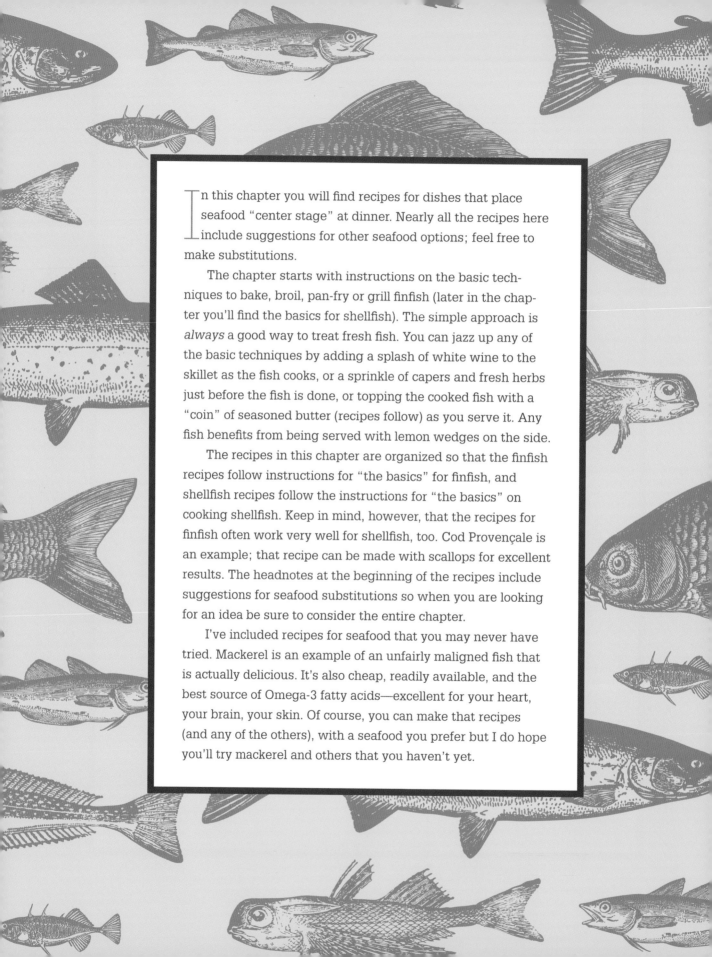

In this chapter you will find recipes for dishes that place
seafood "center stage" at dinner. Nearly all the recipes here
include suggestions for other seafood options; feel free to
make substitutions.

The chapter starts with instructions on the basic techniques to bake, broil, pan-fry or grill finfish (later in the chapter you'll find the basics for shellfish). The simple approach is
always a good way to treat fresh fish. You can jazz up any of
the basic techniques by adding a splash of white wine to the
skillet as the fish cooks, or a sprinkle of capers and fresh herbs
just before the fish is done, or topping the cooked fish with a
"coin" of seasoned butter (recipes follow) as you serve it. Any
fish benefits from being served with lemon wedges on the side.

The recipes in this chapter are organized so that the finfish
recipes follow instructions for "the basics" for finfish, and
shellfish recipes follow the instructions for "the basics" on
cooking shellfish. Keep in mind, however, that the recipes for
finfish often work very well for shellfish, too. Cod Provençale is
an example; that recipe can be made with scallops for excellent
results. The headnotes at the beginning of the recipes include
suggestions for seafood substitutions so when you are looking
for an idea be sure to consider the entire chapter.

I've included recipes for seafood that you may never have
tried. Mackerel is an example of an unfairly maligned fish that
is actually delicious. It's also cheap, readily available, and the
best source of Omega-3 fatty acids—excellent for your heart,
your brain, your skin. Of course, you can make that recipes
(and any of the others), with a seafood you prefer but I do hope
you'll try mackerel and others that you haven't yet.

Basic Baked Fish Fillets or Steaks

If you're short on time or ingredients, you can bake any fish fillet or steak this way with wonderful results. This recipe is easily doubled; if you end up with a two layers of fillets in the baking dish, place the bottom layer skin-side down in the pan and the top layer skin-side up. Place a tablespoon of butter in the bottom of the baking pan and use half of the butter, lemon, and wine between the layers and the other half on top. Do not layer fish steaks; cook in a single layer only.

Serves 2-4

1 pound fish fillets or steaks* (flounder, fluke, cod, pollack, haddock, sea trout, salmon, swordfish, etc.)

2 tablespoons butter, melted

2 tablespoons fresh lemon juice

2 tablespoons dry white wine

2 tablespoons fine plain bread crumbs

1 tablespoon finely chopped fresh flat leaf parsley

Lemon wedges

Preheat oven to 350°F.

Spread half of the melted butter in a 9x13-inch ovenproof dish. Place the fish fillets, skin side down, in the dish in a single layer. Pour the remaining butter evenly over the fish, then the lemon juice and wine. Top with the bread crumbs and place in the oven for 20 minutes, or until the fish is completely cooked and piping hot. Serve immediately, adding some of the juices from the baking pan to each serving. Top each serving with fresh parsley and serve with lemon wedges.

Note: The thicker the fish fillets or steaks, the longer the baking time. Check with a fork for doneness. Undercooked fish does not have as much flavor as thoroughly cooked fish and does not have as flaky and tender a texture.

During the heyday of schooner fishing out of Gloucester, Massachusetts, most of the fish brought in from the "banks" (either Georges Bank or the Grand Banks) was caught by men trawl-fishing in dories—flat-bottomed boats of about fifteen feet in length. Dory fishing was done year-round on the open ocean, nearly 100 miles or more offshore, with two men in each boat. Once the schooner reached the fishing grounds, the dories were launched over the side and the men rowed a mile or two away to set their trawls—lines with baited hooks. Trawls were kept in half barrels and had an anchor on one end and a buoy on the other. It was not unusual for a dory to return to the ship with almost 1,000 pounds of fish, which then had to be gutted, dressed, and salted.

Basic Sautéed Fish Fillets or Steaks

Fish fillets or steaks are delicious with a quick sauté on top of the stove. A cast-iron skillet works best for this technique but any good heavy-bottomed skillet will do fine. The dredge is for fillets; do not dredge fish steaks.

Serves 2–4

⅓ cup unbleached flour

⅓ cup yellow cornmeal

Salt and pepper to taste

1 pound fish fillets or steaks (flounder, fluke, cod, pollack, haddock, sea trout, salmon, swordfish, etc.)

1 tablespoon vegetable oil

1 tablespoon butter

How Much Fish Should You Buy?

A whole fish will generally yield about half its weight in fillets. For instance, a two-pound flounder will yield about 1 pound of fillets.

Three to four ounces of fish per person is usually good for a starter course, and six to eight ounces is usually about right for a main course serving.

Combine the flour and cornmeal, seasoned with a little salt and pepper, in a wide, shallow bowl. Dredge the fish fillets in the mixture.

Heat the oil and butter over medium heat in a large, heavy skillet. When it is hot but not smoking, add the fish fillets or steaks and cook, turning only once, until golden on both sides. (You will know when it is time to turn the fillets by the golden brown edges that appear as the meat becomes whiter and more opaque. If you flip the first fillet a little too early, you'll know to give the others more time.) A 4-ounce flounder fillet takes about 2 minutes per side; a 1-inch thick fish steak takes about 3–4 minutes per side. Serve immediately.

Basic Grilled Fish Steaks

Swordfish, tuna, and salmon steaks are wonderful when cooked over a bed of hot coals on an outdoor grill. (If you don't have a grill, you can use a broiler pan under your broiler, set about 5 inches below the heat source.) Other firm-fleshed fish, such as monkfish, can also be cubed and skewered, or cut in medallions, and grilled. Any fish suitable for grilling can be marinated first to add flavor and to help keep the steaks moist.

Serves 4

2 pounds fish steaks, cut about 1 inch thick

Lemon wedges

Make sure the grilling rack is clean and dry, then give the side that the fish will sit on a light swipe of cooking oil. Set the rack about 6–8 inches above the hot coals. Place the steaks on the rack when it is hot. (Test by flicking a little water at it; if it hisses, it is hot.)

Cook about 4–5 minutes per side (about 8–10 minutes total cooking time per inch), flipping only once. The outside of the steaks should have a seared "crust" and the inside should be completely cooked, piping hot, and juicy. When the steaks are done, immediately transfer to plates and serve. Lemon wedges are the only accompaniment needed.

Note: You can give the steaks a thin coating of mayonnaise before grilling, if desired, for an even juicier steak.

How to Grill Fish Fillets

Fish fillets generally cannot be cooked directly on the grill; the meat becomes too flaky as it cooks and will fall apart (and into the coals) as you turn it. To prevent this mishap, wrap the grill snugly with a layer of heavy-duty foil, oil it lightly, and then pierce it all over with a toothpick. When the grill is hot, lay the fillets on the foil. Be careful not to tear the foil when turning the fish.

Fillets with the skin on are the best candidates for this technique. The skin acts as a net, holding the meat together as it cooks, and preserves the moisture while adding flavor. Mackerel, bluefish, striped bass, and salmon are all good cooked this way.

Remember to remove the scales before filleting fish.

Two Simple Toppings for
Baked, Broiled, Grilled, or Pan-Fried Seafood

Herbed Butter

4 tablespoons of softened butter

1 finely minced garlic clove

2 tablespoons mixed finely chopped fresh herbs (flat leaf parsley, chives, tarragon, basil, marjoram, or cilantro)

Salt and freshly ground black pepper to taste.

Combine all ingredients well. Place the mixture on a sheet of waxed paper or plastic wrap and roll into a log. Chill until the butter is completely hard. Slice thinly and place a "coin" of the herbed butter on top of each fillet or steak right before serving.

Anchovy Butter

4 tablespoons softened butter

1 finely minced shallot

1 anchovy fillet, smashed

1 tablespoon finely chopped fresh flat leaf parsley

Combine all ingredients well. Place the mixture on a sheet of waxed paper or plastic wrap and roll into a log. Chill until the butter is completely hard. Slice thinly and place a "coin" of the herbed butter on top of each fillet or steak right before serving.

Pan-Seared Sea Trout with Tomatoes and Herbs

A quick splash in sesame oil before being baked slowly in the oven with stewed tomatoes and herbs gives this fish an outstanding flavor. Other fish can be substituted for the sea trout—cod, haddock, or hake fillets are excellent choices, as are scallops or salmon, swordfish, or tuna steaks.

Serves 4

2 pounds sea trout fillets

4 tablespoons fresh lemon juice

4 tablespoons sesame oil

1 cup finely chopped onion

4 garlic cloves, finely minced or pressed

3 cups stewed tomatoes, drained and chopped

4 tablespoons chopped fresh flat leaf parsley

2 tablespoons vinegar

2 tablespoons dry red wine

1/4 teaspoon salt

1 teaspoon chopped fresh marjoram

1/2 teaspoon chopped fresh thyme

2 teaspoons sugar

1/3 cup water

Preheat oven to 300°F.

Place the fillets in a wide, shallow glass dish and pour the lemon juice over them. Turn so that both sides get juice on them.

Place the sesame oil in a large, heavy skillet set over medium heat. When the oil is hot but not smoking, add the fish and cook for 1 minute on each side. Remove and transfer to a wide, shallow baking dish.

In the same oil, over medium heat, cook the onion, garlic, and tomatoes for 5 minutes, stirring occasionally. Add the parsley, vinegar, wine, salt, marjoram, thyme, sugar, and water. Cook for another 5 minutes.

Pour the sauce over the fish and place in the middle of the preheated oven. Bake for 20 minutes. Serve immediately.

Pan-fried Flounder with Lemon and Wine Sauce

This dish is a classic and well worth mastering. Often called Flounder Française in Italian restaurants, it creates a melt-in-your-mouth rich lemony sauce.

Even if you use a 12-inch skillet, you may have to cook the fish in batches. Remove the fish as it is done and transfer it to a plate in a warm oven or warming drawer until you are ready to finish it in the sauce.

The cooking is quick once the fish are in the pan so have all the other parts of the dinner menu ready before you start the fish.

Serves 4

3 eggs

4 tablespoons milk

1½ cups flour

Salt and pepper to taste

2 pounds fish fillets (flounder, whiting, or hake)

2 tablespoons olive oil

8 tablespoons butter

1 cup dry white wine

1 cup fresh lemon juice

½ cup chopped fresh flat leaf parsley

Incentive of the "Share"

Commercial fishermen earn a percentage of the value of the catch, called a share. This arrangement means a trip can be boom or bust; there are no financial guarantees for captain or crew—another one of the uncertainties of this business. This system of pay is as old as fishing and is not likely to change. As Sterling Hayden so aptly observed, "How else could such a vast amount of raw work as goes on in the fisheries ever get done?"

In a wide, shallow bowl beat the eggs with the milk. In a separate bowl mix the flour with a little salt and pepper. Dredge the fish in the flour, pressing well to coat, then dip in the egg mixture, and then back in the flour mixture, pressing well again. Set on a platter as they are done.

In a heavy 12-inch skillet heat the oil and butter over medium heat. When it is sizzling hot but not smoking, place the fillets in the pan. Do not crowd; cook in batches if necessary. Cook until golden. Turn once and cook until golden on the other side (about 2 minutes per side). As soon as all the fish has been cooked, add the wine and lemon juice to the pan. (If you have cooked the fish in batches, return all the fish to the pan before adding the wine and lemon juice.) Cover, remove from the heat, and let sit for 5 minutes.

To serve, place a portion of fillets on each plate. Top with sauce and fresh parsley. Serve immediately.

Crispy Herbed Tautog with Honey Mustard Butter

A coating of white cornmeal, rolled oats, and herbs makes a crisp, handsome shell for the fillets. When served, they are topped with little disks of an herbed honey mustard butter that covers the fish as the butter melts—a stunning presentation for a dinner party. Make the honey mustard butter first; it has to chill for at least thirty minutes before using.

This recipe is an adaptation of one from Nancy Carr, executive chef at a lovely waterfront restaurant in South Kingstown, Rhode Island, in the 1990s. Tautog can be difficult to find at your fish market unless you live on the coast but you can substitute hake, whiting, fluke, sea bass or other meaty fish for excellent results.

Serves 6

FOR THE HONEY MUSTARD BUTTER:

6 tablespoons butter, softened

1 tablespoon Dijon mustard

2 tablespoons honey

2 tablespoons finely chopped fresh flat leaf parsley

FOR THE EGG WASH:

2 eggs

2 tablespoons water

¼ teaspoon cayenne pepper

2 tablespoons Dijon mustard

Pinch of salt and pepper

FOR THE CRISPY COATING:

1 cup white cornmeal

½ cup rolled oats (not the "instant" kind)

1 teaspoon dried thyme

1 teaspoon dried basil

1 teaspoon dried marjoram

¼ teaspoon salt

¼ teaspoon freshly ground black pepper

3 pounds tautog fillets

2 tablespoons vegetable oil

2 tablespoons butter

12 lemon wedges

To make the honey mustard butter: Combine the softened butter, mustard, honey, and parsley in a bowl and beat together until thoroughly blended. Transfer to plastic wrap and form into a long log about 1 inch in diameter. Chill in the refrigerator for 1 hour or in the freezer for 30 minutes, until completely firm.

For the fillets: In a wide, shallow bowl beat together the eggs, water, cayenne pepper, mustard, salt, and pepper to create the egg wash.

In a separate bowl combine the cornmeal, oats, herbs, salt, and pepper.

Dip the fillets in the egg wash, then dredge in the cornmeal mixture, pressing to coat well.

In a heavy 12-inch skillet heat the oil and butter over medium heat. When sizzling hot, place the fish fillets in the pan and cook about 4 minutes per side, or until golden, turning only once, and carefully so as not to remove the coating. When the fillets are cooked, transfer to dinner plates. Top each fillet with two nickel-size slices of honey mustard butter. Place two lemon wedges on each plate and serve immediately.

Old-Fashioned Fish and Chips

You can easily make great fish and chips at home even if you don't have a deep-fat fryer. I use a 10-inch cast-iron skillet and fry the fish in a half-inch of vegetable oil.

This is my idea of classic fish and chips: The fish is coated with a batter that forms a crisp jacket around the tender juicy fish inside. We love this made with hake, but there are lots of other fish—haddock, ling, cod, even flounder—that do well in its place. Serve with tartar sauce and coleslaw.

Serves 4

FOR THE BATTER:

1 cup flour

1 teaspoon baking soda

Salt and pepper

3 eggs

6 tablespoons beer

3 tablespoons cider vinegar

3 tablespoons vegetable oil

FOR THE CHIPS:

2 pounds Russet potatoes, peeled and cut into french fry sticks

1½ cups vegetable oil for frying

2 pounds hake or other firm-fleshed fish (see headnote)

Flour for dredging

Note: If you are using a 10-inch skillet, you will need 1½ cups of vegetable oil to cook the fish and chips. If you are using a larger skillet, you will need slightly more to bring the oil to a depth of ½ inch.

To make the batter: In a large bowl sift together the flour, baking soda, and a pinch of salt and pepper. In a separate bowl beat the eggs. Add the beer, vinegar, and oil to the eggs, and beat together well. Add this mixture to the dry ingredients and combine thoroughly. Set aside.

To make the chips: Soak the raw french fry sticks in a bowl of cold water until you are ready to use them. Before frying, dry *thoroughly* with paper towels.

Heat the oil in a 10-inch skillet over medium heat until it reaches 375°F. Add the potatoes, being careful not to splatter hot oil. Cook in batches for about 10 minutes, or until golden outside and tender inside. As the potatoes are cooked, transfer to a cookie sheet lined with brown paper. Sprinkle with salt and place in a warm oven with the heat turned off.

To cook the fish: Dredge each fillet in flour and then dip in the batter. Immediately place the coated fish carefully into the same hot oil in which you cooked the potatoes, still at a temperature of 375°F. Coat only as much fish as you can cook at one time; if you coat it all at once and set it on a platter, the batter will stick to the platter, not the fish. Cook the fish until golden, about 1–2 minutes per side depending on the thickness of the fillet. As the fish is done, use a slotted spatula to transfer it to a cookie sheet lined with brown paper; place it in the oven with the fries. (While you are tending the cooking fish, use a slotted spoon to remove and discard any batter particles that float off the fish and begin to cook. They will burn, and if you leave them in the pan, they will flavor the oil with a burned taste.)

As soon as all the fillets are cooked, serve them with the chips. Place a shaker bottle of cider vinegar and bowls of tartar sauce and lemon wedges on the table.

Pan-fried Crispy Mackerel Fillets

What makes these fillets crispy is a handsome coating of rolled oats. And the oats help offset the natural oiliness of mackerel (it's the good-for-you Omega-3 oil). The finishing touch is a tangy sauce. Make the sauce first to allow the flavors to develop while the mackerel is being prepared and cooked.

Mackerel is often sold whole and is easy to fillet; see page 172 for details. You could substitute bluefish, sea bass, haddock, or fluke if you can't get mackerel

Serves 4

FOR THE SAUCE:

⅓ cup fresh lemon juice

2 tablespoons fresh lime juice

⅓ cup dry white wine

½ bay leaf

1 tablespoon minced onion

2 tablespoons Dijon mustard

1 cup sour cream

1 tablespoon chopped fresh dill

1 tablespoon chopped fresh flat leaf parsley

Salt and pepper to taste

½ cup white cornmeal

Salt and pepper

2 eggs, beaten

2 cups rolled oats (not the "instant" kind)

2 pounds mackerel fillets, skin removed

⅓ cup vegetable oil

To make the sauce: Place the lemon juice, lime juice, wine, bay leaf, and onion in a saucepan over medium heat. Bring to a low simmer and cook until the liquid is reduced by nearly half. In a bowl combine the mustard with the sour cream; add this mixture to the saucepan, whisk, and return to a simmer. Continue cooking for an additional 2 minutes. Stir in the dill and parsley, and remove from the heat. Season to taste with salt and pepper. Set aside.

To cook the fish: Set out three wide, shallow bowls: one for the cornmeal, seasoned with a little salt and pepper; one for the eggs; and one for the oats. Dip each fillet in the cornmeal, then in the egg, and then in the rolled oats, pressing firmly in the oats to create a solid coating. Transfer each fillet to a platter until you have coated all the fillets.

In a large, heavy 12-inch skillet heat the oil over medium heat. When the oil is hot but not smoking, gently place the fillets in the pan and cook for about 3–4 minutes on each side, or until a deep golden color. Turn carefully with a spatula so as not to disturb the coating. When the fish are done, transfer to a platter and serve immediately with the sauce on the side and plenty of fresh lemon wedges.

Fish Cakes

The original edition of this book included a recipe for Salt Cod Cakes, which I love. But in my travels promoting the book, I discovered that (1) salt cod can be difficult to find, and (2) no one is terribly interested in cooking with it anyway. (It is an old-fashioned item that was extremely popular in the nineteenth century, more popular than fresh cod!)

So, here is a recipe for Fish Cakes instead; everyone loves them. These cakes can be made with nearly any fish—including salt cod (as long as you rinse and prepare it according to the direction on the little wooden box it comes in).

I'm certain fish cakes were originally developed as a way to use up leftovers; the fish must be cooked—baked, poached, broiled—before you combine it with the other ingredients and form it into cakes. I often make a double batch and store one batch of formed but not cooked fishcakes in the freezer.

Fishcakes make a very satisfying supper and are good served with a crisp green salad.

Makes 2 dozen

1 pound fish fillets, cooked and flaked (cod, haddock, pollack, whiting, hake, ling, fluke, flounder, salmon— whatever suits your taste)

1 cup diced onion

3 tablespoons vegetable oil

3 cups cooked mashed potatoes

⅓ cup milk

2 eggs, beaten

2 tablespoons softened butter

¼ cup freshly chopped flat leaf parsley

½ teaspoon freshly ground black pepper

Place the flaked, cooked fish in a large mixing bowl. Add the onion, mashed potatoes, milk, eggs, butter, parsley, and pepper, and mix thoroughly with a wooden spoon (or your hands).

Lightly flour your hands and form the fish/potato mixture into patties about 2½ inches to 3 inches in diameter and ¾ inch thick. Heat the remaining 2 tablespoons of vegetable oil in a large skillet over medium heat. When the oil is hot but not smoking, carefully place the cakes in the oil and cook until golden on both sides, about 3–4 minutes per side, turning only once. They should have a crispy gold-brown crust and be piping hot inside. As the fish cakes are cooked, transfer them to a plate in a warm oven until you have cooked them all. Serve hot with fresh lemon wedges.

Cod Provençale

The beauty of this dish is its simplicity. Cod is pan-seared and then surrounded with a classic mix of "Provençale" vegetables—fresh plum tomatoes, onion, garlic, and black olives—to finish together in the pan. You can substitute other meaty white fish for the cod (haddock, tuna, swordfish, monkfish) as well as shrimp (shelled and de-veined but leave the shell intact at the tail). A great recipe to make during the peak of summer.

Serves 4

2 tablespoons olive oil

2 tablespoons butter

²/₃ cup chopped onion

1 garlic clove, finely minced

2 pounds cod fillets

8 plum tomatoes, peeled, seeded, and chopped

8 Kalamata olives or other brine-cured black olives, pitted and chopped

¹/₂ teaspoon chopped fresh thyme

1 tablespoon chopped fresh basil

Place the oil and butter in a large, heavy skillet over medium heat. Add the onion and garlic, and cook, stirring occasionally, until the onion becomes tender and translucent but the garlic is not browned. Remove the vegetables from the pan, return the pan to the heat, and when it is hot but not smoking, add the cod fillets and cook them for about 1 minute.

Return the onion and garlic to the pan with the fish. Add the tomatoes, olives, and thyme, sprinkling them over and around the fish. Turn the heat to medium-low, cover the skillet, and cook for about 3–4 minutes more, or until the fish is cooked thoroughly and the vegetables are tender and juicy.

To serve, place a fillet on each plate and spoon the vegetables over the fish, using all the juices that form in the pan, too. Sprinkle fresh basil over each and serve immediately.

Stuffed Squid

Here is an elegant way to serve squid. The bodies are filled with a savory stuffing, lightly sautéed, and topped with a simple wine sauce. The stuffing can be prepared in advance, and the squid can be stuffed and kept in the refrigerator for up to a day until you are ready to finish the dish.

Serves 4

½ cup olive oil

8 large squid, cleaned and tentacles chopped (see page 177)

¼ cup finely chopped onion

¼ cup finely chopped celery

½ cup finely chopped mushrooms

3 garlic cloves, minced

2 cups fresh bread crumbs

¼ cup chopped fresh flat leaf parsley

Salt and pepper to taste

2 cups dry white wine

Place ¼ cup of the olive oil in a large, heavy skillet over medium heat. When it is hot, add the chopped squid tentacles, onion, celery, mushrooms, and garlic, cooking until tender and fragrant but not browned. Add the bread crumbs and stir until all ingredients are well combined and the bread crumbs are golden. Season to taste with salt and pepper. Remove from the heat and transfer the mixture to a large bowl. Stir in the parsley and set aside.

When the bread crumb mixture has cooled, stuff each squid about three-quarters full (the stuffing will expand when cooked). Close the end of the squid body with a toothpick. If there is any leftover stuffing, you can put some on each plate when you serve the squid.

When all the squid are stuffed, divide the remaining ¼ cup of olive oil between two large skillets and place over medium heat. When the oil is hot, add the stuffed squid bodies and cook, turning, for 1–2 minutes, until the squid begins to turn opaque white with golden edges. Add 1 cup of wine to each pan, lower the heat, and cover. Cook for about 8 minutes more, occasionally basting and turning the squid. Remove the squid from the pans and transfer to serving plates—two stuffed squid per person. Leave the wine mixture uncovered in the warm pans while you cut each squid on the diagonal into three sections. Remove the toothpicks. Pour a little wine sauce over each serving and serve immediately.

Curried Monkfish

When I was a teenager, I had a job as a mother's helper for a woman who was big on what were considered "exotic" recipes then. She taught me how to make a delicious shrimp curry. As I developed recipes for this book, I wanted to reproduce that dish but with an "underutilized" seafood: monkfish. But, feel free to make this dish with any firm white fish, or shrimp or scallops. This recipe yields a lot of sauce, so serve it over nutty brown rice.

For a hotter flavor, increase the amount of curry powder.

Serves 6

2 tablespoons butter

¼ cup minced shallots

1 cup sliced mushrooms

1 cup Madeira wine

2½ pounds monkfish, cut in 1-inch cubes (or other seafood)

1 cup golden raisins

2 tablespoons curry powder (Penzey's Spices makes my favorite)

3 egg yolks, beaten

1½ cups yogurt

In a large 12-inch, heavy skillet melt the butter over medium heat. Add the shallots and mushrooms, and cook until tender but not browned. Add the Madeira and simmer over medium-low heat until the liquid is reduced by nearly half, about 5 minutes. Add the fish, raisins, and curry powder, and continue cooking for about 4 minutes. The monkfish is cooked when it turns white.

In a large bowl beat the egg yolks with the yogurt. Add this to the skillet and stir the mixture gently over medium-low heat until it thickens sufficiently. This will take only a few minutes. *Do not let the mixture boil.* Serve immediately, over rice.

Stuffed Fluke

Fluke is a meaty, flavorful fish, and its fillets lend themselves well to being split and stuffed—the fillets are thick and hold their shape as they bake. This stuffing includes spinach and a few scallops, adding flavor and moisture. The dish can be assembled ahead and kept in the refrigerator until ready to bake, making it an easy but impressive main course for a dinner party.

When shopping for the fish, look for fillets that are about 1-inch thick or, a whole fish of about six pounds (which will yield two large, meaty fillets of a pound and a half each). The fillets can be cut in three sections each, yielding six pieces—one per person

You can also substitute a flounder fillet and roll it around the stuffing.

Serves 6

FOR THE STUFFING:

2 tablespoons butter

²/₃ cup minced onion

1 cup minced celery

2 garlic cloves, finely minced or pressed

1¹/₂ cups fresh bread crumbs

2 teaspoons finely chopped fresh flat leaf parsley

²/₃ cup packed fresh baby spinach leaves, chopped

1 tablespoon fresh lemon juice

2 tablespoons dry vermouth (or white wine), divided

¹/₄ pound shucked scallops, chopped

FOR THE FLUKE:

3 pounds fluke fillets (if the fillets are not think enough to split, roll them around the stuffing)

3 tablespoons butter

2 tablespoons fresh lemon juice

Preheat oven to 350°F.

To make the stuffing: Heat the butter in a large, heavy skillet and add the onion, celery, and garlic. Cook, stirring, over medium heat until the vegetables are tender but not browned. Add the bread crumbs, stir and continue cooking until they are golden. Transfer the mixture to a large bowl. Allow the mixture to cool slightly as you chop the parsley and spinach. Add the parsley, spinach, lemon juice, and 1 tablespoon of vermouth to the bread crumb mixture and toss. Add the scallops and blend thoroughly. Divide the stuffing into 6 equal portions.

To stuff the fish: Using a sharp fillet knife, butterfly each fillet (split each fillet horizontally, leaving one end of the fillet intact so that the split produces a flap, not a new fillet). Place one portion of the stuffing in the opening and gently push the top of the fillet down over it. If the fillets are thin, roll them around the stuffing.

Place the stuffed fillets in a baking pan. Top each with a half tablespoon of the butter and pour the lemon juice and remaining vermouth over all. Cover the pan with foil and bake for 25 minutes, or until done. Serve immediately.

Broiled Bluefish with Anchovy Vinaigrette

It seems counterintuitive that a strong-flavored oily fish (like bluefish) would be well complimented by another strong-flavored oily fish (like anchovy)—but it is! The bite of anchovy and vinegar in this recipe really enhance the sometimes one-note quality of bluefish. As a matter of fact, the anchovy sauce compliments almost any fish so do try this recipe with other varieties of seafood.

Serves 4

2 pounds bluefish fillets (or any other fish of your choice)

1/4 teaspoon freshly ground black pepper

1/4 teaspoon salt

1/2 teaspoon grated lemon zest

6 anchovy fillets

2 teaspoons Dijon mustard

1/2 cup chopped fresh flat leaf parsley

3 teaspoons fresh lemon juice

3 teaspoons white wine vinegar

6 tablespoons olive oil

Preheat the broiler.

Place the fillets, skin side down, on a broiler pan lined with foil.

In a small bowl combine the pepper, salt, and lemon zest. Reserve 1/4 teaspoon and use the rest to rub over the fillets.

Place the remaining ingredients in a blender along with the reserved pepper/lemon zest mixture. Puree until the anchovies and parsley are finely minced.

Place the fish under the broiler, no closer than 6 inches, and broil without turning for 12–15 minutes, until completely cooked.

Remove the fish from the oven and transfer with a spatula to plates. Top with the anchovy sauce and serve immediately.

Broiled Fish with Red Pepper Pesto

Virtually any fish will do well in this recipe so start with your favorite and then try another the next time. The roasted red pepper "pesto" can be made in advance and kept in the refrigerator until needed. Bring to room temperature before using. Make this when there is an overabundance of sweet red bell peppers at your local farmers' market.

Serves 4

2 red bell peppers, roasted (see page 5)

4 tablespoons grated Parmesan cheese

4 tablespoons olive oil

1 tablespoon chopped fresh flat leaf parsley

1 tablespoon fresh lemon juice

2 pounds fish fillets of your choice

Salt and pepper

To make the red pepper pesto: Skin and seed the roasted red peppers and finely chop. This should yield about 1 cup; reserve ¼ cup. Place all but the reserved pepper in a large bowl with the cheese, oil, parsley, and lemon juice. Mix together well and transfer to a food processor or blender. Pulse until the mixture is slightly smoother but not completely pureed. Transfer to a mixing bowl and stir in the reserved ¼ cup of chopped pepper. Set aside.

To cook the fish: Preheat the broiler. Place the fillets in a broiler pan and sprinkle a little salt and pepper over each. Cook under the broiler, 6 inches from the heat source, until done, about 8 minutes (longer for thicker fillets, less time for thinner fillets). The meat should be piping hot and flakey.

Transfer to individual plates and top each portion with a generous dollop of red pepper pesto. Serve immediately.

Broiled Mackerel with Mustard Butter

The tangy mustard butter sauce is the perfect contrast to the rich taste of mackerel, and it's quick and easy to prepare. If you can't get mackerel, try this recipe with bluefish, salmon, or tuna steaks. Make the mustard butter ahead of time.

Serves 4

FOR THE MUSTARD BUTTER:

1 tablespoon Dijon mustard

2 tablespoons butter, softened

2 tablespoons finely chopped fresh flat leaf parsley

2 tablespoons fresh lemon juice

FOR THE MACKEREL:

2 pounds mackerel fillets

1 tablespoon oil

Salt and pepper

1/2 tablespoon butter, cut in bits

2 tablespoons fresh lemon juice (about 1 lemon; do not use anything but fresh)

To make the mustard butter: Mix all the mustard butter ingredients together in a small bowl. Cover and refrigerate for at least 30 minutes.

To broil the mackerel: Preheat the broiler. Place the fillets, skin side down, in a broiler pan. Brush the tops with the oil and sprinkle with a little salt and pepper. Distribute the butter over the fillets. Place under the broiler, 6 inches from the heat source, and cook for 5–8 minutes, or until done. Remove from the oven and immediately pour the lemon juice over the fillets. Transfer to plates.

Top each serving with a generous teaspoon of the mustard butter and serve immediately.

Fish Baked with Basil Pesto

Basil pesto makes a great partner for baked fish, and you can use nearly any fish you like. You can buy commercially prepared pesto but it's easy to make; try the recipe on page 168.

Serves 4

2 pounds fish fillets

¼ cup water

¼ cup dry white wine

¾ cup Basic Basil Pesto (page 168)

½ cup fresh bread crumbs

1 tablespoon chopped fresh flat leaf parsley

¼ teaspoon paprika

¾ cup thinly sliced onion

2 tablespoons fresh lemon juice

1 tablespoon butter, cut in bits

Preheat oven to 425°F.

Place the fillets, skin side down, in a baking pan in a single layer. Add the water and wine to the baking pan. Spread the basil pesto evenly over the fillets.

In a small bowl mix together the bread crumbs, parsley, and paprika. Sprinkle this mixture evenly over the pesto-topped fillets. Top the bread crumbs with the onion slices. Sprinkle with lemon juice and dot with butter.

Place in the preheated oven and bake for 20 minutes, or until the fish is completely cooked and piping hot. Serve immediately, pouring some of the cooking juices over each serving.

How to Freeze Seafood

Most seafood can be frozen without detriment to its taste or texture. First wrap it well in wax paper or plastic wrap and then in heavy-duty foil, pressing out any air pockets as you go. Fold and seal the edges of the foil securely. Label the package with the contents, their weight, and the date. Then place the package in an airtight plastic freezer bag, seal, and store. (This last step helps prevent freezer burn and keeps fish odors from invading the ice cubes, ice cream, and other items in your freezer.)

When you are ready to use it, remove the wrapping and place the frozen block of seafood on a wide glass plate, cover, and let sit in your refrigerator overnight or up to 24 hours. The microwave is not a good way to defrost frozen seafood; even on low settings it can cook the edges and dry the fish.

For best results use fish within a month of freezing it.

Roasted Whole Sea Bass

Sea bass, when cooked, has a white meat that literally gleams. It is tender, juicy, and flavorful. An easy fish to fillet, it is also a good candidate for baking whole: the meat lifts nicely off the bone, and the tender skin is edible or, if you prefer, easily pushed aside. The two things this technique has going for it are ease of preparation and the extra flavor gained by cooking on the bone.

You can use this technique for roasting other whole fish, but for larger fish increase the liquid ingredients and the cooking time.

Serves 4

4 whole sea bass, about ½ pounds each

Salt and pepper

4 sprigs of fresh rosemary, about 4 inches long

8 sprigs of fresh thyme, about 4 inches long

8 sprigs of fresh flat leaf parsley

1 lemon, thinly sliced

1 tablespoon olive oil

4 tablespoons fresh lemon juice

1 cup dry white wine

3 tablespoons butter, cut in bits

Preheat oven to 400°F.

Trim any sharp fins from the fish. Scale, gut the fish, and remove the gills. Rinse quickly under cold running water. Rub the cavity of the fish with salt and pepper, and then stuff each with 1 sprig of rosemary, 2 sprigs of thyme, and 2 sprigs of parsley. Stuff 2 or 3 lemon slices, halved, into the cavities with the herbs. Rub the fish with olive oil and place in a lightly buttered baking pan. Pour the lemon juice and wine over the fish. Dot with the butter and place in the middle of the oven. Bake for 25–30 minutes, until the meat is white and completely cooked.

Lift the fish out of the baking pan onto a platter and with a paring knife make an incision behind the head and at the tail. Then gently, with a small spatula, lift the fillet off the bones. Turn the fish over and repeat the process. Divide the fillets among the plates and pour the sauce from the baking pan over all. Serve immediately.

Monkfish Kebabs

Monkfish meat is firm and easily cubed, making it an excellent fish for the grill. Be sure to remove the skin; it is inedible. You can substitute large cubes of tuna steak, jumbo shrimp, or large scallops for the monkfish.

This recipe requires that the fish and vegetables marinate for at least two hours before grilling.

Serves 6

FOR THE MARINADE:

1½ cups olive oil

1½ cups vegetable oil

¾ cup red wine vinegar

¼ cup fresh lemon juice

1 tablespoon Worcestershire sauce

3 garlic cloves, crushed

1 tablespoon chopped fresh basil

1 tablespoon chopped fresh parsley

1 teaspoon chopped fresh dill

Salt and pepper to taste

FOR THE KEBABS:

4 medium-size onions, cut in quarters

3 bell peppers, cut in chunks

18 large mushrooms

18 cherry tomatoes

2 small zucchini cut in ½-inch-thick slices

2 pounds monkfish, cut in generous 1-inch cubes

Whisk together all the marinade ingredients. Place the cubed monkfish in a large bowl and ladle approximately 1 cup of marinade over the fish. Gently toss the fish to coat; cover the bowl with plastic wrap and refrigerate.

Place the vegetables in a separate bowl and cover with the remaining marinade. Toss gently. Cover with plastic wrap and refrigerate. (If you find the vegetables have more than sufficient marinade, add the extra to the fish.)

Arrange the vegetables evenly on skewers, using some of each on every skewer. Place the monkfish on separate skewers. Place the kebabs on a hot clean grill and cook, turning frequently, for 10–15 minutes. The fish should be opaque throughout, but be careful not to overcook.

Serve immediately.

Note: When grilling kebabs, always marinate seafood and vegetables separately, and discard the seafood marinade when you put together the kebabs. Baste the kebabs sparingly during the grilling; too much marinade will cause the coals to flame. If using bamboo skewers, soak them in cold water for about 15 minutes before threading the ingredients onto them. Kebabs cook faster than steaks and may need only a few minutes.

Soy and Ginger Grilled Tuna Steaks

Use this recipe for tuna steaks or, cubed tuna on skewers. You can also substitute swordfish, monkfish, salmon or shrimp for the tuna.

Serves 4–6

2 pounds tuna steaks

FOR THE MARINADE:

½ cup soy sauce

½ cup dry sherry

2 tablespoons vegetable oil

4 tablespoons finely minced fresh ginger root

2 teaspoons sugar

2 garlic cloves, finely minced or pressed

Combine the marinade ingredients in a bowl and whisk together well. Place the tuna in a single layer in a glass baking pan. Pour the marinade over the tuna, cover, and refrigerate for at least 1 hour, turning and basting the meat after 30 minutes.

To cook, place steaks in a lightly oiled grill pan or on a grilling rack set about 8 inches above the hot coals of an outdoor grill. Cook for about 5 minutes per side. When done, the meat will flake apart. Serve immediately.

Note: Discard the marinade when you cook the fish.

Superstitions

Fishermen hold to a number of superstitions not familiar to the rest of us. Here are some of the more common ones:
Don't turn a hatch cover upside down.
Don't whistle, it whistles up a breeze.
Don't mention "pig" on board.
Don't shave on a trip.
Don't leave for a trip on a Friday.
Don't return a knife in any way other than it was given.
Don't put your hat in your bunk.
Thirteen-pot trawls are bad luck.
Don't leave the dock twice in the same day.
Don't take women on a trip.
Don't brag, it brings bad luck.
Don't serve beef stew aboard; it brings on a gale.

Seafood Tacos

Everybody loves tacos, which is why we have adapted them in all kinds of ways from their Mexican origins. Here, chunks of marinated and pan-grilled seafood are layered along with fresh tomato, avocado, onion, lettuce, cheese, and salsa, and stuffed into a crisp taco shell to make a delicious and a fun meal-in-one-dish. The seafood options are nearly endless: shrimp, swordfish, or monkfish all work well but you can expand your seafood options considerably. Experiment and see what you like in a seafood taco! Have all the other ingredients ready before you cook the fish.

Serves 4 (2 tacos per person)

1 pound fish (cut in 1-inch cubes if using monkfish or swordfish)

FOR THE MARINADE:

½ cup olive oil

¼ cup fresh lime juice

2 teaspoons fresh lemon juice

2 tablespoons finely chopped fresh cilantro

1 garlic clove, finely minced or pressed

1 jalapeño pepper, finely minced

Salt and pepper

FOR THE VEGETABLE FILLING:

2 ripe avocados, peeled, pits removed, and chopped

2 cups diced tomatoes

2 cups shredded lettuce

1 cup chopped red onion

1 tablespoon finely chopped fresh cilantro

1 teaspoon fresh lime juice

Salt and pepper

½ cup sour cream

8 large taco shells

½ cup grated Monterey Jack cheese

1 cup salsa (as hot as you like)

To marinate the fish: Combine all the marinade ingredients in a large bowl. Add the fish and toss well. Cover and refrigerate for at least 1 hour.

To cook the fish: Cook the marinated fish in a lightly oiled and hot grill pan over medium heat, turning, until the fish is golden and completely cooked. Transfer to a platter.

To make the tacos: In a large bowl combine the avocado, tomatoes, lettuce, onion, cilantro, and lime juice. Toss and season to taste with salt and pepper.

Spread a little sour cream down the center of each taco. Place a portion of the vegetable mixture over that. Top with some seafood, a little grated cheese, and a tablespoon of salsa. Place two tacos on each plate and serve immediately, with more salsa on the side.

Basic Boiled or Steamed Shellfish

For many people this technique yields the absolute best results. It is also exceedingly simple.

The steps for steaming lobster, crab, shrimp, clams, or mussels are virtually the same. The cooking time varies, and the cooking liquid can be seasoned. Clams and mussels must be scrubbed well with a stiff brush under cold running water before cooking, and mussels must be de-bearded.

You need a very large pot with a lid to steam shellfish (I use one that's 14-inches in diameter by 11-inches tall). For shrimp, clams, or mussels it is helpful but not necessary to have a pot with a set-in, removable strainer.

The cooking liquid from clams and mussels makes excellent fish stock for soups and sauces. You can save the liquid from shrimp if it is not too highly seasoned.

Basic Steps:

Put cold water (or other cooking liquid) in the pot to a depth of 2 inches. Add seasonings if using.

Bring the water to a boil over high heat.

When the water reaches a boil, add the shellfish and cover the pot tightly. Note: The pot can be crowded but do not layer lobsters more than two deep or crabs more than three deep. Instead, use two pots.

When water returns to a boil, set the timer.

When the cooking time is complete (see chart on page 106), remove the pot from the heat, then remove the shellfish from the pot. Use tongs for lobsters and crabs, and a slotted spoon for shrimp, clams, and mussels (unless you have a pot with a removable strainer). Set lobsters and crabs in a colander to drain and cool for 1–2 minutes before serving. Serve shrimp, clams, and mussels immediately.

To save the broth from clams or mussels for fish stock: Place the uncovered pot over high heat, bring to a boil, reduce the heat and simmer for 5 minutes. When cool, pour the broth through a fine-mesh sieve lined with a double layer of dampened cheesecloth into a glass container with a lid. Refrigerate until ready to use. Otherwise, place in a freezer container and store in freezer until ready to use.

The "Basics" for Shellfish

The shellfish harvested in the water off New England is some of the best in the world. Our lobsters are considered a delicacy in places as far away as Norway and Japan. Many people visiting coastal New England look forward to a boiled lobster dinner with as much excitement as they do any other part of their trip.

SHELLFISH	COOKING TIME
Lobsters of 1½ pounds each	12 minutes
Cooking Liquid:	
Water	
Rock Crabs of 1 pound each	10 minutes
Cooking Liquid:	
Water	
½ cup vinegar and/or beer	
1 bay leaf	
¼ teaspoon whole black peppercorns	
2 tablespoons hot red pepper flakes	
Shrimp, medium	5 minutes
Cooking Liquid:	
Water	
2 tablespoons fresh lemon juice	
½ teaspoon cayenne pepper	
¼ teaspoon dry mustard	
1 bunch celery leaves	
Clams or Mussels	5 minutes
Cooking Liquid:	
Equal parts water and dry white wine	

Serving Tips: At each place setting have a bowl of lemon wedges and a bowl of melted butter or cocktail sauce or strained broth. For lobster or crab, you'll need to provide tools (nut crackers, lobster shears, lobster picks, and crab forks). Lots of napkins are necessary (some people like bibs) because eating shellfish out of the shell is a messy affair. Set a large bowl in the center of the table to hold the empty shells.

Lobster, crab, and shrimp are also good served cold, with lemon wedges, cocktail sauce, or homemade Herbed Mayonnaise (page 165).

Lobster: After the cooked lobsters have cooled for a minute or two, split them down the stomach and tail with a sharp knife and crack the claws in a couple of places before serving.

Crab: After the cooked crabs have cooled for a minute or two, set them on a board and give them a rap with a kitchen mallet in a couple places before you serve them.

Clams or mussels: When the cooking time is complete, use a slotted spoon or tongs to remove the ones that have opened (this should be most of them) and place in a colander set over a bowl. Cover the pot again and allow the unopened clams or mussels to cook for another minute or two. Discard any that do not open.

Basic Sautéed Shellfish

This technique is perfect when you want to do something quick and simple with scallops or shrimp.

Serves 4

1 tablespoon olive oil

1 tablespoon butter

**1¼ pound shucked scallops or peeled and deveined
  shrimp**

Heat the oil and butter in a large, heavy skillet over medium heat. When the butter is sizzling, add the scallops (or shrimp) without crowding the pan. After about a minute, use a metal spatula to loosen a scallop (the first crust they form will stick to the pan and you want to keep it attached to the scallop) and turn it with tongs. If it has developed a nice golden crust, you can turn all the scallops. Continue cooking and turning the scallops until they have a golden crust on all sides, 4–6 minutes total depending on the size. Serve immediately, with lemon wedges.

Note: Shrimp will cook a little faster than scallops and will not develop as much of a crust, but they should have some golden edges.

How and When to Rinse Seafood

Before you begin preparing a recipe with shellfish that you have purchased shucked, such as scallops or clams, check the seafood for grit and shell fragments. One of the best ways to do this is with a quick rinse in salt water: Fill a large glass mixing bowl with fresh cold water and add 4 tablespoons of salt for every quart of water. Stir well. Place the seafood in the salted water and gently swirl with your hands. Quickly and carefully remove the seafood to a clean linen towel or double layer of paper towels set over a rack; gently pat dry.

If you will be using the liquid the shellfish was packed in, such as oysters or clams, strain it through a fine-mesh sieve lined with a double layer of dampened cheesecloth.

The other occasion to consider giving fish a "bath" is when seafood that *should* be fresh is smelly, which can happen with improper storage. Before you toss it out, see if it can be salvaged with a rinse. Follow the steps listed above; if the seafood still has an unpleasant odor, you must discard it. Often, however, the bad smell will disappear and the fish will be almost odorless, as truly fresh seafood is.

Basic Grilled or Broiled Shellfish Kebabs

Shucked scallops and oysters, and peeled and deveined shrimp, can be skewered and cooked on a hot grill over an outdoor fire or under a broiler.

Marinating for an hour or two is the best way to prepare shellfish for the grill, but you can skip that step if you're in a big hurry.

Serves 4

1¼ pounds shucked scallops or oysters*
or cleaned shrimp

Bamboo skewers soaked for 15 minutes in cold water

Marinade (see page 100) or 2 tablespoons olive oil

Thread the shellfish on the skewers, barely touching. Brush them with marinade or olive oil. Place on a clean, lightly oiled grilling rack set about 8 inches above the hot coals or under a broiler. Cook, turning, until all sides are golden. Or, place them in a broiler pan about 6-inches from the heat source and cook, turning until all sides are golden, approximately 5–7 minutes total cooking time, depending on the size of the meat on the skewer. Serve with lemon wedges.

Note: Because oysters are so soft, it is usually best when cooking them on skewers to wrap them with a piece of partially cooked bacon or to sandwich them between chunks of vegetables.

How to Store Seafood

Fresh filleted or shucked seafood should be refrigerated in covered glass containers until you are ready to cook it. Fish stays fresher longer when sitting in glass rather than plastic. This is particularly noticeable with certain seafood such as scallops, which will quickly become slimy and develop a bad odor when stored in a plastic bag or container. Stored in glass, however, scallops stay sweet and fresh for days.

Basic Grilled or Broiled Shellfish in the Shell

Clams and oysters can be broiled or grilled in their shells; as they cook, their shells open. Serve them hot or cold, with lemon wedges or cocktail sauce, or with Herbed Mayonnaise (page 165). (Live crabs and lobsters can also be cooked on a grill over a hot fire, but I have never found that method very satisfactory.)

Makes 24

12 oysters in the shell (flat side of shell facing up)

12 littleneck clams in the shell

2 tablespoons melted butter

2 tablespoons fresh lemon juice

To broil: Scrub the oyster and clam shells well with a stiff brush under cold running water. Place side by side on a cookie sheet and place under a hot broiler about 6 inches from the heat source. Cook until the shells begin to open, 4–6 minutes. Remove from the oven, and when cool enough to handle, remove and discard the top shells. Dribble a little melted butter and lemon juice over each and return to the oven to broil for an additional 1–2 minutes, or until the juice in the shells is bubbling.

Note: Place the oysters flat side up for either cooking method. Then you have the deeper shell left to hold the oyster and juices.

To grill: Set the oysters and clams on the grilling rack about 6 inches above the heat source. Cover with a lid or foil. After about 4 minutes, lift the lid and check to see if the top shells have opened. Follow the directions above.

Mussels Steamed in Wine and Herbs

This is my version of Moules Marinière, that marvelous and simple French dish. The mussels are served in their handsome blue-black shells along with a fragrant broth. Serve this dish with hunks of a good crusty bread to soak up the juices at the bottom of the soup bowl.

Serves 4

6 pounds live mussels (shells of about 2-2 ½ inches)

2 cups dry white wine

1 large garlic clove, minced

¼ cup minced shallot

½ teaspoon chopped fresh thyme

1 bay leaf

2 tablespoons butter, cut in bits

⅓ cup chopped fresh flat leaf parsley

Clean the mussels by scrubbing them well under cold running water. De-beard using your thumb and index finger to grasp and pull the little tangle of brown "hairs." (It's not hair but that's what it looks like, which is why it's called a "beard".)

Place the wine, garlic, shallot, thyme, and bay leaf in a large stockpot. Bring to a boil, lower the heat, and simmer for 10 minutes. Add the mussels, cover the pot, and raise the heat to high. Cook for 3–5 minutes, until all the shells have opened. (Discard any that do not open.)

With a slotted spoon transfer the mussels to four large soup bowls. After the last mussel is out of the pot, raise the heat, add the butter, and stir (it will melt almost immediately). When the butter has melted, remove the pot from the heat, stir in the parsley, and ladle the liquid into the soup bowls, using all the broth. Serve immediately.

Spicy Cajun Shrimp

A mix of spices and beer make a dark, thick sauce around the shrimp—very flavorful and perfect over rice.

Serves 4

2 teaspoons cayenne pepper

1 teaspoon black pepper

1 teaspoon crushed red pepper

½ teaspoon salt

1 teaspoon dried thyme

2 teaspoons dried basil

1 teaspoon dried oregano

⅔ cup butter

3 garlic cloves, minced

2 teaspoons Worcestershire sauce

2 cups diced tomato

2 pounds medium shrimp, peeled and deveined

½ cup beer, at room temperature

4 cups cooked rice

In a small bowl combine the three peppers, salt, thyme, basil, and oregano.

Place the butter in a large 12-inch skillet over medium heat. Add the spice mixture, garlic, and Worcestershire sauce, and stir. When the butter is melted, add the tomato. Place the shrimp over the tomatoes and cook, stirring occasionally, for about 2 minutes. Pour in the beer, cover, and cook at a simmer for another minute, or until the shrimp are pink with golden edges. Remove from the heat.

To serve: Place some rice on each plate and top with a portion of shrimp and sauce. Serve immediately.

Crab Cakes

Crab cakes make a wonderful main course for lunch or dinner. Serve them with a green salad or coleslaw and, if you like, a dollop of Herbed Tartar Sauce (page 167).

For a memorable Sunday Brunch, make eggs Benedict using crab cakes instead of Canadian bacon: Place the poached eggs on the hot crab cakes and top with Blender Hollandaise sauce (page 166). Yum!

Make these as mini-crab cakes and serve as an hors d'oeuvres.

Makes eighteen 3-inch cakes

2 pounds fresh lump crabmeat

¼ cup finely chopped fresh flat leaf parsley

¼ cup minced onion

½ cup minced celery

¼ cup minced green bell pepper

1 cup corn kernels (fresh or frozen, thawed)

1 garlic clove, finely minced or pressed

2 cups fresh bread crumbs

3 eggs, beaten

3 tablespoons melted butter, cooled

⅓ cup milk

1 teaspoon Worcestershire sauce

2 tablespoons fresh lemon juice

½ teaspoon paprika

¼ teaspoon cayenne pepper

¼ teaspoon salt

½ cup cornmeal

Vegetable oil

Pick over the crabmeat for shell fragments and place in a large bowl. Add the parsley, onion, celery, bell pepper, corn, and garlic, and mix together. Add the bread crumbs and toss to distribute evenly.

In a separate bowl whisk together the eggs, butter, milk, Worcestershire sauce, lemon juice, paprika, cayenne pepper, and salt.

Add the egg mixture to the crab mixture and combine thoroughly. Form into 3-inch cakes, sprinkle each side with cornmeal, and transfer to a cookie sheet. (If the mixture is not moist enough to form cakes, add a little milk.) Cover with plastic wrap and refrigerate for at least 1 hour.

When ready to cook, pour vegetable oil into a large, heavy skillet to a depth of ¼ inch. Heat the oil over medium heat, and when it is hot, add the crab cakes and cook them until golden on both sides (about 4 minutes per side), turning carefully with a spatula only once. You will probably have to cook the crab cakes in batches; as they are done, transfer to a platter in a warm oven. Serve hot.

Oyster Bread Pudding

This is a creamy, chock-full-of-oysters bread pudding, enhanced by onions, red peppers, and mushrooms caramelized in rendered bacon fat—midwinter comfort food at its best. Add a Romaine lettuce salad, pour some wine, and settle in for the evening.

This recipe is an adaptation of a favorite from the Gatehouse Restaurant in Providence, Rhode Island.

Serves 4–6

2 strips bacon

1 tablespoon olive oil

1 cup thinly sliced onion rings

⅔ cup finely diced red bell pepper

1 cup sliced mushrooms

2⅔ cups milk

1 cup light cream

2 bay leaves

½ teaspoon chopped fresh thyme

½ teaspoon chopped fresh marjoram

Pinch of salt and pepper

5 eggs

2½ cups shucked oysters, coarsely chopped (with ½ cup liquid reserved for this recipe)

5 cups bread cubes from top-quality French or Italian bread (cut roughly into ½ inch to 1 inch cubes)

Preheat oven to 350°F.

In a large, heavy skillet cook the bacon until it is crisp and has rendered its fat. Remove the bacon and transfer it to brown paper to drain; when it has cooled, crumble and set aside. Add the olive oil to the bacon fat and place over medium heat. When hot, add the onion, stir once, and turn the heat to low. Cover and cook for 10 minutes, occasionally removing the cover to stir. Add the red pepper and mushrooms, and continue cooking over low heat, covered, occasionally removing the cover to stir, for an additional 10 minutes.

In a heavy saucepan combine the milk, cream, bay leaves, thyme, marjoram, salt, and pepper. Scald over medium heat, then set aside to cool.

In a large bowl beat the eggs well. When the scalded milk has cooled, remove and discard the bay leaves and add the milk to the eggs, whisking well. Add the oysters, ½ cup of their liquid, bread cubes, and caramelized vegetables. Mix gently but thoroughly with a spoon, cover, and refrigerate for 30 minutes.

Pour the mixture into a buttered 2-quart soufflé dish. Set the dish in a wide baking pan, and pour water into the baking pan so that it reaches about halfway up the sides of the soufflé dish. Place in a preheated oven, being careful not to let the water slosh into the pudding, and bake for 50–60 minutes, until the top is golden and the pudding has begun to pull away from the sides of the dish. Remove the soufflé dish from the baking pan and set on a cooling rack; let sit for 3 minutes, and serve.

Note: For an elegant first course, bake the puddings in individual buttered custard cups. Reduce the baking time by about 10 minutes. (This recipe would fill twelve custard cups, so for a party of six, halve the recipe.)

Crab Soufflé

This soufflé is creamy and light inside with a delicate crust on top, and a wonderful crab and tarragon flavor throughout.

Soufflés are not as hard to make as you may think. You do need a soufflé dish, because the straight sides are important for proper rising, and you can't have people running through the kitchen slamming doors, jumping up and down, or otherwise creating a ruckus. This will cause the soufflé to "fall" while it's still in the oven.

A soufflé will collapse slightly when you serve it, but don't let this concern you. Be sure, however, to have everything else you'll be serving with the soufflé ready to go before you take it out of the oven. Take it right to the table so your guests can see how pretty it is. The sooner you serve it, the better.

Makes one 9-inch soufflé

Butter to grease soufflé dish

3 tablespoons grated Parmesan cheese

4 tablespoons butter

3 tablespoons minced scallions

4 1/2 tablespoons flour

1 1/2 cups milk

6 eggs, divided, plus an additional egg white

2/3 cup grated Fontina cheese

4 teaspoons fresh lemon juice

1 1/2 teaspoons Dijon mustard

Salt and pepper to taste

1 cup cooked crabmeat (about 1/2 pound)

2 tablespoons finely chopped fresh tarragon (or 1 1/2 teaspoons dried, crushed)

1/4 teaspoon cream of tartar

Thoroughly butter a 2-quart soufflé dish and sprinkle with the Parmesan cheese, tilting the dish so that it is evenly coated.

Preheat oven to 400°F.

Melt 4 tablespoons of the butter in a large saucepan over medium heat. Add the scallions and cook until tender but not browned. Sprinkle in the flour and stir until it is incorporated with the butter. Gradually add the milk, stirring constantly, and allow the mixture to thicken each time before adding more milk. When all the milk has been added and the mixture is thick, remove from the heat and whisk in the egg yolks, one at a time. Add the cheese, lemon juice, mustard, salt, and pepper, stirring well. Add the crabmeat and tarragon, and mix until completely blended. Transfer to a large bowl.

In a large, deep glass bowl beat the egg whites until foamy. Add the cream of tartar and continue beating until they are stiff but not dry.

Gently fold the beaten egg whites into the crab mixture (not the other way around) but do not beat them in—fold gently. The little clusters of stiff egg white are what will make the soufflé rise properly. Pour gently into the prepared soufflé dish. In the indentation at the top of the dish, run your thumb around the edge of the soufflé, creating a little groove.

Place in the middle of the oven, lower the heat to 375°F, and bake for about 40 minutes, or until the top of the soufflé is puffy and golden and the sides are coming away from the dish. Serve immediately.

Lobster Pie

This is a simple, old-fashioned treat with a single flaky pastry crust on the bottom, a filling of chunks of lobster nestled in a creamy cheddar sauce, and a top crust of fresh herbed bread crumbs.

When my husband was a lobsterman, from 1985 to 1992, I had many occasions to find uses for leftover lobster. This is one of the recipes I developed. Like all recipes, consider it a starting point. My sister Jane likes to make this dish without the bottom crust—it's still a winner!

Makes one 9-inch deep-dish pie

FOR THE FILLING:

2 tablespoons butter

2 tablespoons minced shallots

1 garlic clove, finely minced or pressed

2 tablespoons unbleached flour

1¼ cups milk

¼ cup dry white wine or vermouth

Salt and pepper to taste

1½ cups grated cheddar cheese

1 pound cooked lobster meat, coarsely chopped

FOR THE TOPPING:

2 tablespoons butter

1 cup fresh bread crumbs

1 teaspoon chopped fresh flat leaf parsley

½ teaspoon chopped fresh thyme

1 garlic clove, finely minced or pressed

Pinch of salt and freshly ground black pepper

1 Basic Pie Crust (page 163), fitted into a 9½-inch deep-dish pie plate and blind-baked

To make the filling: In a large, heavy skillet melt the butter over medium heat. Add the shallots and garlic, and cook until tender and fragrant but not browned. Sprinkle with the flour and stir until the flour is incorporated in the butter. Slowly whisk in the milk, allowing the mixture to thicken slightly each tine before adding more. After all the milk has been added and the sauce is fairly thick, add the wine and continue stirring and cooking until the mixture thickens again. Add the grated cheese and stir gently until the cheese melts. Remove from the heat and add the lobster meat. Set aside.

To make the bread crumb topping: Melt the butter in a large skillet over medium heat. Add the bread crumbs, parsley, thyme, garlic, salt, and pepper, and toss lightly until the bread crumbs are golden. Remove from the heat and set aside.

Preheat the oven to 350°F.

To assemble the pie: Pour in the lobster filling into the blind-baked and cooled pie shell, and top with an even layer of the herbed bread crumbs. (At this point it may look as if you should have used a regular pie plate, but you need the deep-dish plate so the filling won't bubble up over the edges as it bakes.)

Bake in the preheated oven for 45 minutes, or until the pastry is golden and the top is bubbling. Remove from the oven, transfer to a rack, and let sit for a few minutes before cutting into wedges to serve.

Lobster Facts

- A lobster is the size of a mosquito when it is born.
- A lobster is approximately seven years old before it weighs a pound and is legal to keep.
- As a lobster grows, it sheds its shell, increasing in weight by twenty-five percent each time. It will go through this process, known as molting, twenty to thirty times before it reaches one pound.
- A lobster's age is approximately its weight multiplied by four, plus three years.
- Lobsters eat fish, other crustaceans, and mollusks.
- Lobsters live on the ocean floor and store food by burying it; they will defend the food stash much as a dog does.
- A one-clawed lobster is called a cull and is less expensive than a lobster with both claws intact.

How to Select and Store Live Lobsters and Shellfish

Look for lively lobsters—ones that are actively moving about in the tank. Soft-shelled lobsters are just as tasty as hard-shelled lobsters; the shell is soft because it's new.

Transport your lobsters home in a sturdy bag or empty cooler, covered with a layer of newspaper, and put them in the crisper drawer of your refrigerator as soon as you get home. Do not store them in water or crushed ice! They will keep in a crisper drawer for a day or so. The cool temperature puts them in an almost dormant state, but when you remove them from the refrigerator, they should start to move around. Never cook crabs or lobsters that have died! Instead, bury them deep in your garden or compost pile.

CHAPTER 7

Vegetables

Recipes

Corn Pudding

Potatoes Anna

Spinach Soufflé

Balsamic Green Beans

Sautéed Broccoli Rabe

Stewed Swiss Chard

Fried Green Tomatoes

Eggplant Salad

Zucchini Pancakes

Classic Potato Salad

Creamy Coleslaw

Kevin's Caesar Salad

Rice Salad

Farro and Green Bean Salad

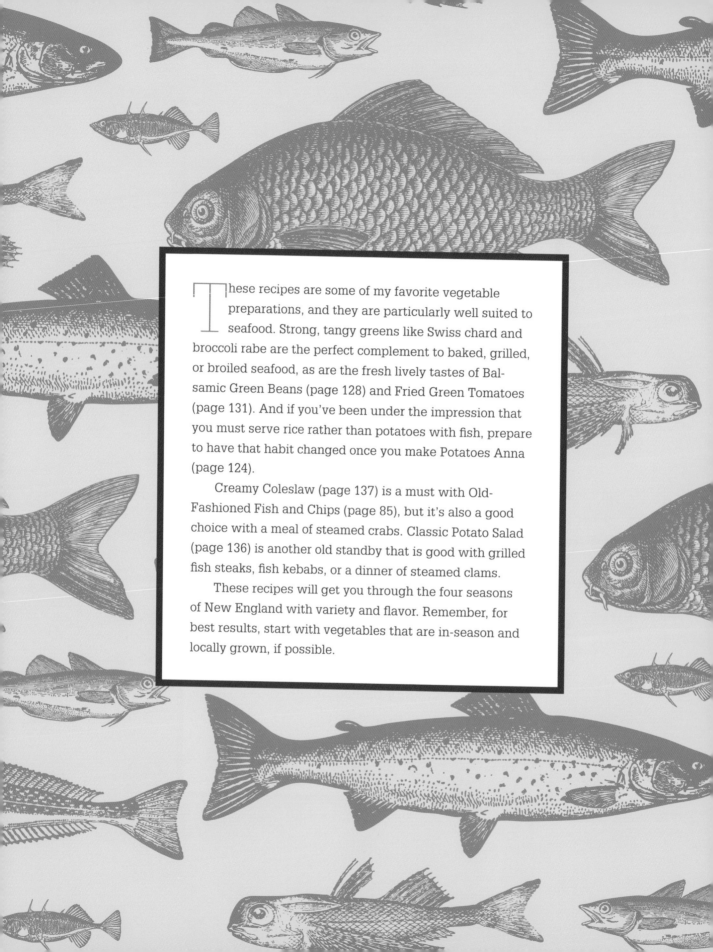

These recipes are some of my favorite vegetable preparations, and they are particularly well suited to seafood. Strong, tangy greens like Swiss chard and broccoli rabe are the perfect complement to baked, grilled, or broiled seafood, as are the fresh lively tastes of Balsamic Green Beans (page 128) and Fried Green Tomatoes (page 131). And if you've been under the impression that you must serve rice rather than potatoes with fish, prepare to have that habit changed once you make Potatoes Anna (page 124).

Creamy Coleslaw (page 137) is a must with Old-Fashioned Fish and Chips (page 85), but it's also a good choice with a meal of steamed crabs. Classic Potato Salad (page 136) is another old standby that is good with grilled fish steaks, fish kebabs, or a dinner of steamed clams.

These recipes will get you through the four seasons of New England with variety and flavor. Remember, for best results, start with vegetables that are in-season and locally grown, if possible.

Corn Pudding

This recipe is the heart of simplicity and a very traditional New England dish. You can make it in the summer when fresh corn is at its peak, and in the winter with frozen corn. Either way, it's a winner.

Serves 4

3 cups fresh corn kernels (or frozen, defrosted
   but not cooked)

2 eggs, beaten

1 cup milk

1 teaspoon sugar

Salt and pepper to taste

Preheat oven to 350°F.

In a blender or food processor combine 1 cup of corn kernels with the rest of the ingredients and pulse until the corn is pureed. Transfer the mixture to a bowl and stir in the rest of the corn by hand. Pour into a buttered 9x13-inch baking dish and bake for 30–35 minutes. Remove from the oven, let sit for a minute on a cooling rack, cut into squares, and serve.

Love for the Challenge

Every day's different—there is no monotony for people who really love fishing.
—Phil Schwind,
Cape Cod Fisherman

Potatoes Anna

The bottom layer of this dish becomes its crisp golden top when served—bring the dish to the table because it makes a very pretty presentation. Layers of thinly sliced potatoes almost melt together as they cook, transforming the whole into something much greater than the sum of its three parts. For best results, use a cast-iron skillet.

A food processor is the best way to slice the potatoes thinly and consistently. If you do this step ahead of time, store the potatoes in a bowl of water in the refrigerator to keep them from turning brown.

Serves 6

4 tablespoons butter (3 tablespoons cut into small bits)

8 cups peeled and thinly sliced (1/8 inch) russet potatoes

Salt and pepper

Preheat oven to 350°F.

Melt 1 tablespoon of the butter in a lightly oiled 10-inch cast-iron skillet (or other heavy, ovenproof skillet) over medium heat. As soon as the butter is sizzling but not browned, quickly place a thin layer of overlapping potato slices in the skillet. Sprinkle with a little salt and pepper and a few bits of butter. Repeat this process until you have used all the potatoes, ending with a topping of a little salt and pepper and bits of butter. You should be able to complete the layering in about 3 minutes, giving the potatoes a total of about 4 minutes on top of the stove (it's this step that creates the crisp golden crust); if it's taking you longer than 3–4 minutes, leave the skillet on the burner but turn off the heat.

Place the skillet in the middle of the preheated oven and bake, uncovered, for about 40 minutes, or until the potatoes are completely tender (test with a cake skewer, thin knife, or toothpick).

Remove the skillet from the oven. Run a flexible knife around the edge to loosen any areas that are stuck to the sides. Place a flat, heat-resistant 12-inch round serving plate over the skillet. Wearing an oven mitt on each hand, hold the serving plate tight against the skillet and carefully invert it. The Potatoes Anna will fall out onto the plate in one whole cake-like form, revealing a beautiful golden top. Allow the dish to sit for a minute or two. Use a sharp knife to cut into wedges, and serve.

018008 FISH FLAKES, GLOUCESTER MASS.

Up until the middle of the nineteenth century, salting was the primary method of preserving fish. Acres of land were devoted to the use of drying salted fish on "flakes," long wooden slatted platforms on which the salted fish was placed to dry. Elevated coverings of boughs or longs strips of cloth were used to keep the rain off, positioned to allow some direct sun to hit the fish as that gave it the "best color." Construction and placement of the flakes was an art and a science, with the goal being flakes that allowed the sun to dry the fish with the aid of northwest winds. Properly dried salt cod would resist spoilage for at least nine months.

Spinach Soufflé

This soufflé is made with frozen spinach, and comes together quickly in a food processor. It comes out of the oven puffy and golden, with a bit of a crust on the top and a creamy, airy filling. Feta cheese adds a savory bite.

Serves 6–8

2 10-ounce boxes frozen chopped spinach

6 eggs, beaten

4 tablespoons butter, melted

1/2 pound Swiss cheese, grated

1/2 pound feta cheese, crumbled

1/4 teaspoon nutmeg (optional)

Preheat oven to 350°F.

Cook the spinach according to the directions on the package. Transfer to a colander and allow to drain, then wrap in paper towels and squeeze out all the water. Return the spinach to the colander and set aside.

In a large bowl or a food processor fitted with the metal blade, combine the eggs, butter, cheeses, and nutmeg; mix thoroughly. Add the spinach and pulse until blended.

Spoon the mixture into a buttered 9x13-inch baking dish and bake for 30 minutes. Cut into squares and serve immediately.

Balsamic Green Beans

This recipe may change your mind about green beans, which are all too often served over-cooked and soggy.

Serves 4-6

2 pounds fresh green beans, washed but not trimmed

1 tablespoon olive oil

2 tablespoons minced shallots

1 garlic clove, finely minced or pressed

2 tablespoons balsamic vinegar

Salt and pepper to taste

Bring a large pot of lightly salted fresh cold water to a boil over high heat. Add the beans and when the water returns to a boil cook the beans, uncovered, for exactly 1 minute, no longer. Drain immediately into a colander and place the colander under cold running water, or plunge it into a bowl of ice water for a minute, to stop the cooking. Set the cooled beans aside in the colander to drain completely.

Remove the stem ends of the beans (and the strings if there are any), and cut the beans in thirds (each piece will be a little over an inch long). Lay the cut beans on paper towels while you continue with the recipe.

In a large, heavy skillet heat the olive oil over medium heat. When the oil is hot but not smoking, add the shallots and cook until tender but not browned. Add the garlic, stir, and cook until the garlic is fragrant but not browned. Add the green beans, toss lightly, and continue cooking for about 3 minutes, until the beans are thoroughly hot. Add the balsamic vinegar to the pan, toss quickly, and remove from the heat. Season to taste with salt and pepper, and serve immediately.

Sautéed Broccoli Rabe

If you've never had broccoli rabe, the best way I can describe the flavor is a cross between broccoli and arugula. It is tangy and delicious and very high in vitamin C. Wonderful with seafood.

Serves 4-6

2 pounds fresh broccoli rabe

2 tablespoons olive oil

2 garlic cloves, finely minced or pressed

2 tablespoons fresh lemon juice

Freshly ground black pepper to taste

Clean the broccoli rabe under cold running water, removing any tough stem ends and leaves that have yellowed. Bring a large pot of lightly salted cold water to a boil. Add the broccoli rabe, and when the water returns to a boil, cook, uncovered, for 2 minutes. Drain in a colander and place under cold running water, or plunge it into a bowl of ice water for a minute, to stop the cooking. Set the cooled broccoli rabe aside in the colander to drain.

Heat the olive oil in a large, heavy skillet over medium-low heat. Add the garlic, stir, and cook briefly, until just fragrant. Raise the heat to medium; add the broccoli rabe and stir to coat it thoroughly with the oil. Cook over medium heat, tossing occasionally, for about 4 minutes, or until it is tender but not soft. Turn off the heat, and add the lemon juice, toss; remove the pan from the heat and top with a generous grind of black pepper, toss again and serve immediately.

Stewed Swiss Chard

Swiss chard, like all the dark green leafy vegetables, is a nutritional powerhouse. It is tangy yet smooth in taste, and its rich green color offers a lively contrast to seafood, which is mostly pale in color.

Chard is easy to grow and an attractive addition to the garden. If you have the space, put in a short row; you'll be well rewarded.

It is important to the success of this recipe to dice and mince the vegetables finely; they are for flavor, and their texture should hardly be apparent.

Serves 4

10 cups tightly packed, cleaned Swiss chard

2 tablespoons olive oil

1/3 cup finely diced carrot

1/3 cup finely diced onion

2 garlic cloves, finely minced

1/2 cup tomato sauce

1/2 cup dry red wine (Cabernet Sauvignon is good)

Remove and discard any tough stems and ribs from the chard (or save them for a vegetable stock). Wash the chard as you would lettuce and spin dry in a lettuce spinner or spread on paper towels and pat dry. Tear into large pieces and set aside.

Place the olive oil in a large, heavy skillet over medium heat. When hot but not smoking, add the carrot and onion, and cook, stirring occasionally, until soft and tender but not browned. Add the garlic and continue to cook, stirring, just until the garlic is fragrant—do not allow the garlic to brown. Add the tomato sauce and wine, and bring to a simmer. Stir and simmer over medium-high heat for a few minutes, then add the chard and cover the skillet with a tight-fitting lid. Turn the heat to the lowest setting and cook for 3 minutes. Raise the lid, stir the chard, and cover; cook for another 10 minutes. Remove the lid and continue cooking, uncovered, for 3–5 minutes to allow some of the liquid to evaporate. Stir the chard one last time and serve hot.

Fried Green Tomatoes

Crisp on the outside, juicy and tangy on the inside—fried green tomatoes are great with seafood. If you grow your own tomatoes, you can make this recipe often, from the time tomatoes start ripening until well into the fall. Or, ask your greengrocer to get you some if there aren't any for sale with the red tomatoes.

I like to use a green tomato that has just the faintest beginning of an orange blush on it. These are more flavorful and juicy than the solid green ones.

Serves 4–6

6 large green tomatoes

1 cup buttermilk

³/₄ cup unbleached flour

²/₃ cup yellow cornmeal

¹/₂ teaspoon salt

¹/₂ teaspoon freshly ground black pepper

**1 tablespoon (or more as needed) vegetable oil
    or bacon fat**

Slice the tomatoes ¼ inch to ⅜ inch thick. Set aside on a plate.

Pour the buttermilk into a wide, shallow bowl. In a separate bowl combine the flour, cornmeal, salt, and pepper. Working with one tomato slice at a time, dip each into the flour mixture, then the buttermilk, and then the flour again, pressing to coat the slice well. Set them in a single layer on a large platter until you are finished.

Heat the oil or bacon fat in a large, heavy skillet (cast iron is best) over medium heat. When the oil is hot but not smoking, carefully place some tomatoes in the pan without crowding them and cook until golden on both sides, turning only once with a spatula. As they are cooked, transfer to a platter or cookie sheet covered with brown paper and set in a warm oven with the heat off. Repeat until all the slices are cooked. If necessary, add additional vegetable oil or bacon fat to the skillet as the batches require. Serve immediately.

Eggplant Salad

In the summer, it's nice to get your cooking done early in the day, while it's cool. Good news: this salad should be prepared in the morning to allow the flavors to develop. Serve with dinner as is or on a bed of torn crisp Romaine lettuce. It's good with any seafood, prepared any way but we particularly like it with grilled fish steaks.

Serves 4.

1 large eggplant, cut into ½" cubes

FOR THE DRESSING:

5 tablespoons olive oil

2 tablespoons red wine vinegar

1 garlic clove, minced

¼ teaspoon dried thyme

¼ teaspoon dried oregano

1 tablespoon lemon juice

FOR THE TOMATOES:

Salt and black pepper

¼ cup chopped flat leaf parsley

1 red bell pepper, minced

1 cup cherry tomatoes, chopped

½ cup pitted Greek olives, rough chopped

1 cup crumbled feta cheese

Preheat oven to 375°F

Coat a shallow baking pan with 1 tablespoon of the olive oil. Spread the eggplant cubes onto the pan, and toss so that each piece is lightly coated with oil. Bake for approximately 10–15 minutes, or until the cubes are tender (test one with a fork). Remove from stove and transfer pan to a cooling rack.

While the eggplant cools, whisk together the remaining olive oil, vinegar, garlic, dried herbs, lemon juice, and salt and pepper to taste in a large bowl. Add the warm eggplant cubes and toss well. Cover the bowl with plastic wrap and let sit at room temperature for 1 hour. Refrigerate if you will not be serving the salad now. Remove from the fridge 15–20 minutes before finishing the dish to allow it to return to room temperature.

To finish the eggplant salad: Add the parsley, red pepper, cherry tomatoes and olives to the eggplant. Toss together gently. Top each serving with crumbled feta cheese.

Zucchini Pancakes

These little pancakes are tender and savory, and a great way to use zucchini if your garden is being overrun by it. Try them with any grilled or baked fish, and serve with wedges of garden-ripe tomatoes, and a dollop of sour cream.

Serves 4–6 (makes about a dozen)

4 cups grated, unpeeled zucchini

½ teaspoon salt

4 eggs

1 cup crumbled feta cheese

½ cup chopped onion

1 tablespoon chopped fresh basil

1 teaspoon chopped fresh flat leaf parsley

1 teaspoon fresh lemon juice

¼ teaspoon freshly ground black pepper

⅓ cup flour

1 tablespoon (or more as needed) olive oil

The Oldest Profession

Fishing is a form of hunting, and since humans were hunters before they were cultivators, it is one of the oldest occupations in the world.

Place the grated zucchini in a colander set in a bowl. Sprinkle with ½ teaspoon of salt and toss lightly with your hands. Let sit for 15 minutes, then press with your hand until no more liquid comes out of zucchini. Wrap the zucchini in paper towels and squeeze well; more liquid will come out. When the zucchini is completely dry, return it to the colander and set aside.

Beat the eggs well in a large bowl. Stir in the feta cheese, onion, basil, parsley, lemon juice, and pepper. Sprinkle the flour into the mixture and combine well. Add the zucchini and stir until all the ingredients are thoroughly combined.

Heat the oil in a large, heavy skillet over medium heat. When the oil is hot but not smoking, drop the batter by spoonfuls into the hot skillet without crowding (two generous tablespoons of batter per pancake). Cook the pancakes over medium heat, turning only once, until golden on both sides. If you are cooking them in batches, transfer the cooked pancakes to a warm platter. Serve hot, with lemon wedges and sour cream.

Note: It's time to flip the pancakes when little bubbles form in the top of the uncooked side, indicating that the bottom is done. When you flip it, the bottom should be golden. Give the second side slightly less time to cook than the first side. Do one as a tester, cutting into it to check the center if you are unsure.

Classic Potato Salad

This is my version of the potato salad my parents taught me to make. I offer it here with two dressing choices: a traditional mayonnaise dressing and a warm bacon vinaigrette. If you are going to use the mayonnaise dressing, this can be made up to a day in advance; the salad will improve if it is allowed to sit for at least a couple of hours before serving. The warm vinaigrette dressing gives the salad an entirely different effect; that version should be served right away.

Serves 6

FOR THE SALAD:

2¹/₂–3 pounds russet or red-skinned potatoes, washed and quartered

³/₄ cup chopped red onion

¹/₂ cup chopped celery

1 cup diced and quartered cucumber (seeded and partially peeled)

¹/₂ cup chopped gherkins (small pickles)

¹/₄ cup chopped fresh flat leaf parsley

2 tablespoons chopped fresh basil or dill

FOR THE MAYONNAISE DRESSING:

1 cup mayonnaise

1 tablespoon fresh lemon juice

1 teaspoon Dijon mustard

Salt and pepper to taste

FOR THE VINAIGRETTE DRESSING:

5 slices bacon

¹/₃ cup olive oil

1 teaspoon Dijon mustard

¹/₃ cup cider vinegar

1 teaspoon sugar

Salt and pepper to taste

To make the salad: Cook the potatoes, covered, in a steamer set over boiling water for about 10 minutes, or until completely cooked but not mushy. Set aside to cool.

Peel the cooled potatoes (unless they are very tender red-skinned potatoes, in which case you can leave the skin on) and cut into bite-size chunks. In a large bowl toss together the potatoes, onion, celery, cucumber, gherkins, and herbs. Toss with the mayonnaise or vinaigrette dressing.

To make the mayonnaise dressing: In a small bowl whisk together the mayonnaise, lemon juice, and mustard. Season to taste with salt and pepper. Pour over the salad and toss to coat thoroughly. Cover the bowl tightly with plastic wrap and refrigerate until ready to serve. Allow the salad to sit at room temperature for 10 minutes before serving if you have chilled it.

To make the vinaigrette dressing: Cook the bacon in a skillet until it is crisp. Remove from the pan and transfer to paper towels or brown paper. Add the olive oil, mustard, vinegar, and sugar to the pan with the bacon fat and bring to a simmer. Stir until the sugar is dissolved. Remove from the heat and season to taste with salt and pepper.

Crumble the bacon and add to the salad ingredients. Pour the warm dressing over the salad and toss gently to coat evenly. Serve immediately.

Creamy Coleslaw

Coleslaw is a must with fish and chips but it is also a good choice with lots of other seafood meals, including lobster salad rolls, pan-fried flounder, or broiled mackerel, to name just a few. Make this at least one hour before you plan on serving it to allow the flavors to develop and the cabbage to soften.

Serves 6

6 cups shredded green cabbage

2 cups shredded red cabbage

1 cup grated carrot

1 cup mayonnaise

¼ cup white or cider vinegar

1 tablespoon sugar

1 teaspoon Dijon mustard

Salt and pepper to taste

In a large bowl toss the cabbages and carrot together until evenly mixed.

In a small bowl whisk together the mayonnaise, vinegar, sugar, and mustard. Season with salt and pepper.

Pour the dressing over the vegetable mixture and toss gently until all is evenly coated. Cover the bowl tightly with plastic wrap. Refrigerate for at least 1 hour, or up to 6 hours, before serving.

Commercial fishermen spend much of their time at sea sorting the fish they catch—standing, kneeling, and working with both hands—while the boat rolls and heaves. No wonder they're so strong!

Kevin's Caesar Salad

This is one of my husband's signature dishes. It's great all alone or with just about anything, including baked, grilled, broiled, or fried seafood. He got the recipe from his dad, who got it from the originator, Caesar Cardini, at Caesar's restaurant in Tijuana, Mexico, when eating there one night.

Serves 4

1 large head romaine lettuce

6 flat anchovy fillets, drained and cut in half

²/₃ cup Parmesan cheese

1 cup Garlic Croutons (page 169)

FOR THE DRESSING:

2 garlic cloves

6 flat anchovy fillets, drained

¹/₂ teaspoon Worcestershire sauce

2 eggs*

4 tablespoons fresh lemon juice

²/₃ cup olive oil

Freshly ground pepper to taste

Salt to taste

Trim, wash, and dry the lettuce. Tear the leaves into large pieces, wrap in barely dampened paper towels, and set aside.

To make the dressing: Using a mortar and pestle (or blender), mix together the garlic and anchovies.

Transfer the paste to a bowl, add the Worcestershire sauce, and stir. Set aside.

In a small bowl beat the eggs with the lemon juice. Allow to sit for 5 minutes, then beat again. Add the anchovy mixture and olive oil to the eggs and whisk together well. Add some freshly ground pepper and a pinch of salt.

To assemble the salad: Place the lettuce in a large salad bowl. Add the anchovy fillets to the lettuce and toss.

Pour the finished dressing over the lettuce and toss to coat well. Sprinkle in the Parmesan cheese and toss again. Add the croutons, toss, and serve immediately.

*Note: Use pasteurized eggs if you are concerned about using raw eggs.

Rice Salad

Rice goes well with seafood dishes, and this rice salad is a perfect choice during the summer. Make it in the morning to serve that evening to allow the flavors to develop. Serve at room temperature. Sprinkle a few diced cherry tomatoes on each serving if you like.

Serves 4-6

1½ cups long-grain brown rice, cooked according to
directions on package

½ cup chopped scallions

½ cup chopped celery

½ cup chopped Kalamata olives

⅓ cup extra-virgin olive oil

¼ cup fresh lemon juice

1 teaspoon minced fresh oregano
(or thyme, marjoram, or basil)

3 tablespoons finely chopped flat leaf parsley

Salt and freshly ground black pepper to taste

1 cup crumbled feta cheese

In a large bowl, combine the cooled cooked rice with the scallions, celery, and olives. In a separate bowl combine the olive oil, lemon juice, and herbs. Pour over the rice mixture and toss well. Season to taste with salt and pepper. Add the feta cheese and toss again. Cover and refrigerate until ready to serve. Bring to room temperature before serving.

Farro and Green Bean Salad

Farro is a grain that cooks quickly and can be used in a variety of ways. It goes well with seafood, and has wonderfully chewy texture. Its taste is unique; I describe it as a cross between brown rice and walnuts. Make this salad ahead and serve at room temperature.

Serves 4-6

1 cup farro

**12 ounces green beans, trimmed,
    cut into 1¹/₂-inch pieces**

3 ears corn

3 scallions, thinly sliced

2 tablespoons white wine vinegar

2 tablespoons minced shallot

1 teaspoon Dijon mustard

1 tablespoon minced fresh marjoram

¹/₂ teaspoon kosher salt

1 cup goat cheese, crumbled

Bring a large saucepan or stockpot of salted water to a boil. Add farro and simmer for 20 minutes, or until tender. Drain and pour into a bowl.

Use the same pot of boiling water and blanch the green beans for 3 minutes, or until tender. Rinse under cold water.

In the meantime, cut the corn kernels from the cobs. Add them to the farro, and stir in the scallions and green beans.

In a separate bowl, mix vinegar, shallots, mustard, marjoram, and salt to form a vinaigrette. Pour over the farro mixture and toss gently. Add the goat cheese, and toss again.

Serve slightly chilled or at room temperature.

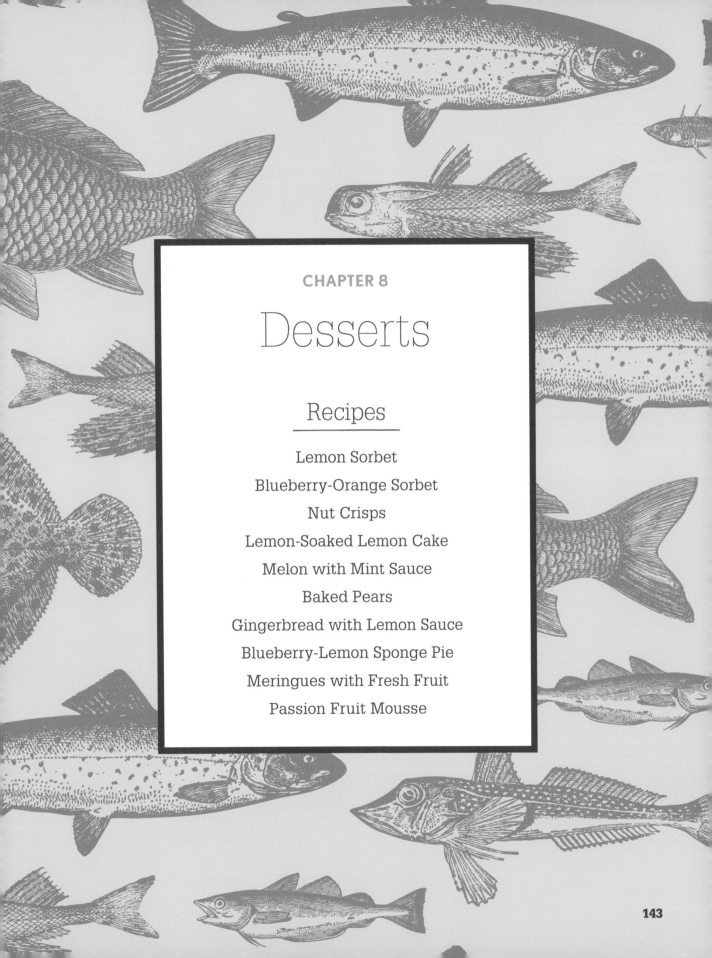

CHAPTER 8

Desserts

Recipes

Lemon Sorbet

Blueberry-Orange Sorbet

Nut Crisps

Lemon-Soaked Lemon Cake

Melon with Mint Sauce

Baked Pears

Gingerbread with Lemon Sauce

Blueberry-Lemon Sponge Pie

Meringues with Fresh Fruit

Passion Fruit Mousse

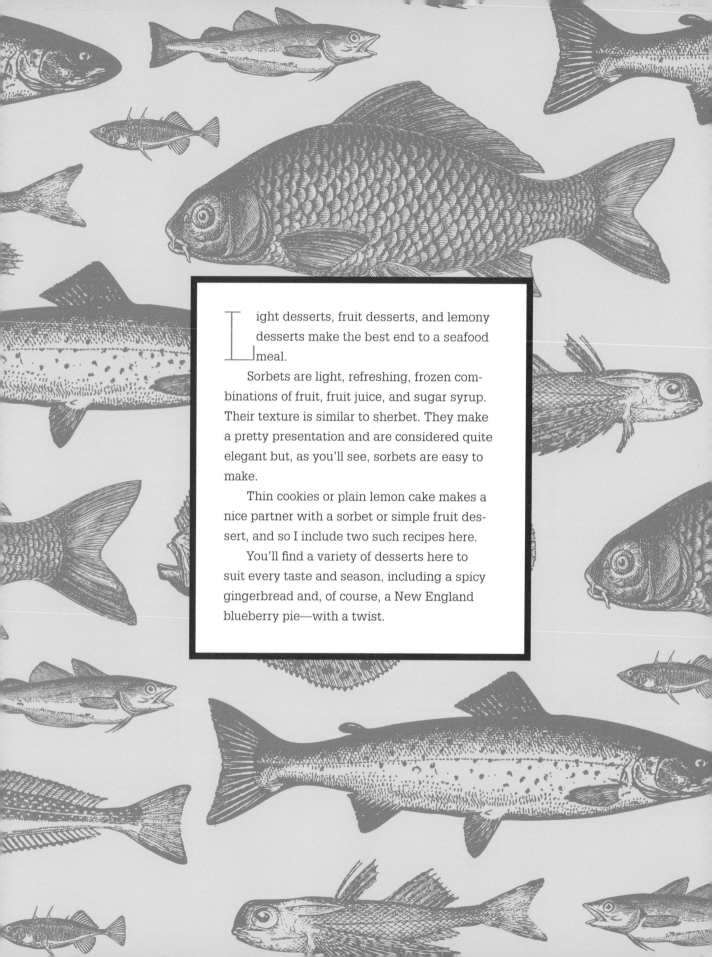

Light desserts, fruit desserts, and lemony desserts make the best end to a seafood meal.

Sorbets are light, refreshing, frozen combinations of fruit, fruit juice, and sugar syrup. Their texture is similar to sherbet. They make a pretty presentation and are considered quite elegant but, as you'll see, sorbets are easy to make.

Thin cookies or plain lemon cake makes a nice partner with a sorbet or simple fruit dessert, and so I include two such recipes here.

You'll find a variety of desserts here to suit every taste and season, including a spicy gingerbread and, of course, a New England blueberry pie—with a twist.

Lemon Sorbet

This is the quintessential dessert to end a seafood meal—lemony, light, and refreshing. I like to infuse the sugar syrup with sprigs of fresh lemon verbena or mint (both hardy herbs here in New England), but they are not necessary.

Serves 4–6

1 cup water

1 cup sugar

¼ cup loosely packed fresh lemon verbena or mint leaves (optional)

¾ cup fresh lemon juice

1 teaspoon grated lemon zest

Combine the water and sugar in a saucepan over medium heat. Add the herbs, if desired. Stir and bring the mixture to a boil. Lower the heat and simmer for 5 minutes. Using a slotted spoon or strainer, remove and discard the herbs. Place the syrup in the refrigerator for at least 2 hours, or until well chilled.

Remove from the refrigerator and stir in the lemon juice and zest. Place in a shallow metal pan, cover with foil, and freeze overnight. Before serving, break the sorbet into chunks, place in a food processor fitted with the metal blade, and pulse quickly until you have the consistency you want. If the sorbet becomes too soft, return it to the freezer for about 10–15 minutes. Serve in footed glass dishes.

The lure of boats and the waterfront is too hard for some to resist, despite many determined parents' plans to the contrary.

Blueberry-Orange Sorbet

Make this when blueberries are in season. Serve with Nut Crisps (opposite).

Serves 4-6

¹/₂ cup water

³/₄ cup sugar

4 cups fresh blueberries

¹/₂ cup fresh orange juice

In a small saucepan combine the water and sugar, and bring to a boil. Lower the heat and simmer for 5 minutes. Cover and refrigerate for at least 2 hours, or until well chilled.

Puree the blueberries and orange juice in a food processor or blender. Pour the mixture through a fine-mesh sieve to remove any solids. Cover and chill for 30 minutes.

Combine the sugar syrup and pureed blueberry mixture. Place in a shallow metal pan, cover with foil, and freeze overnight. Before serving, break the sorbet into chunks, place in a food processor fitted with the metal blade, and pulse quickly until you have the consistency you want. If the sorbet becomes too soft, return it to the freezer for about 10–15 minutes. Serve in footed glass dishes.

Sorbet

Sorbet makes a wonderful dessert all by itself, but it also can be used as a topping for fresh summer fruit—peaches, nectarines, grapes, melons, or any kind of berry.

Sorbet can be flavored with herbs and spices, wines and liqueurs, and countless combinations of fruit. If you want to try inventing some of your own, remember these two rules: (1) too much sugar can inhibit freezing, as can alcohol; and (2) use seasonal fruit at its peak—a flavorless fruit will produce a flavorless sorbet.

Nut Crisps

These thin, buttery cookies are perfect alongside dishes of fruit sorbet. They are baked in the manner of bar cookies and then scored into squares when the pan comes out of the oven. Hello, easy!

Makes about 24 cookies

1 cup butter (2 sticks), softened

1 cup sugar

1 egg, separated

1 teaspoon vanilla extract

2 cups sifted unbleached flour (King Arthur is best)

1 cup finely chopped nuts (pecans, walnuts, or almonds)

Preheat oven to 375°F.

Cream together the butter and sugar until smooth and light. Beat in the egg yolk and vanilla extract. Add the flour and mix until it is incorporated. Pat the dough evenly into a greased jellyroll pan.

Beat the egg white with a fork. Brush it over the top of the dough; sprinkle the nuts evenly over the dough and press them in gently, using your hands or a rolling pin.

Bake for 15–18 minutes, or until golden. Place the pan on a cooling rack and let sit for 10 minutes. Using a sharp knife cut into 1x2-inch bars. Allow the cookies to cool completely before removing from the pan with a metal spatula. Store in an air-tight glass, ceramic, or metal container.

Lemon-Soaked Lemon Cake

This cake is baked in a bread loaf pan, soaked with a lemon glaze when it comes out of the oven, and then sliced like bread. Serve alone or with mixed summer berries, cold poached peaches, grilled plums, or ice cream. Simple and delicious.

Makes one 5x9-inch loaf

FOR THE CAKE:

8 tablespoons butter

1 cup sugar

2 eggs, beaten

1¼ cups sifted unbleached flour (King Arthur is best)

1 teaspoon baking powder

¼ teaspoon salt

½ cup milk

½ cup very finely chopped almonds

1 teaspoon grated lemon zest

FOR THE GLAZE:

2 tablespoons sugar

Juice of 1 lemon

Preheat oven to 350°F.

Cream together the butter and sugar until smooth and light. Beat in the eggs. In a separate bowl combine the flour, baking powder, and salt. Alternately add the flour mixture and the milk to the butter/sugar mixture, beating after each addition. Add the nuts and lemon zest, and blend thoroughly.

Pour the batter into a greased 5x9-inch loaf pan. Bake for 35–45 minutes.

Just before the cake is due to come out of the oven, combine the sugar and lemon juice for the glaze. When the cake is done, transfer the pan to a cooling rack. Using a toothpick, poke holes all over the top of the cake. Stir the glaze well and pour it evenly over the warm cake. Let the cake sit in the pan for 10 minutes, then carefully turn it out of the pan to cool completely on the rack. When cooled, wrap in plastic wrap and chill thoroughly before serving.

Melon with Mint Sauce

This dessert is as refreshing to your eyes—beautiful shades of cool green—as it is in your mouth. The list of ingredients appears too plain to yield anything special, but don't be fooled. This is another dish where the whole is greater than the sum of its parts. If you want to really wow your guests, peel the grapes.

Serves 4

1 large ripe honeydew melon

2 cups sweet green grapes, seedless (optional: peeled)

Juice of 2 oranges

Juice of 1 lemon

1 tablespoon finely chopped fresh mint

2 tablespoons sugar

Sprigs of mint for garnish

Halve the melon and remove the seeds. Using a melon baller, scoop the flesh into a large bowl. Be sure to squeeze the rinds over the melon balls when all the melon has been removed; there is usually a lot of juice clinging there.

Halve the grapes lengthwise and add to the melon. In a small bowl combine the orange and lemon juices, mint, and sugar. Pour over the fruit and toss gently with a spoon. Cover the bowl tightly with plastic wrap and refrigerate for at least 1 hour to allow the flavors to develop.

Allow the bowl to sit at room temperature for 5 minutes before serving. Toss the fruit gently and serve in footed glass dishes, adding any juices that are left in the bottom of the bowl, and top with a sprig of mint if desired.

Baked Pears

This simple preparation yields exquisite results. You can assemble the dish in advance and keep it in the refrigerator until you are ready to bake it.

Serves 4

4 ripe Anjou pears, halved, cored, and peeled

1/2 teaspoon cinnamon

1/4 teaspoon nutmeg

4 tablespoons butter, softened

4 tablespoons brown sugar

1 tablespoon fresh lemon juice

Whipped cream or frozen vanilla yogurt for topping

Preheat oven to 350°F.

Place the pears in a buttered pie plate, arranged like the spokes of a wheel with the narrow ends pointed toward the center, cored surface facing up.

In a small bowl combine the other ingredients thoroughly. Cover and chill for about 15 minutes, or until the mixture is a thick paste.

Dividing the mixture evenly among the pears, fill each cavity (created when the core was removed). Spread the rest over the remaining surface of the pears.

Bake for 20 minutes. Serve warm, topped with whipped cream or frozen vanilla yogurt.

"He pared buckets of potatoes, . . . chopped cabbage, baked huge loaves of bread, . . . pies, cookies, and cakes . . ."

The cook has always been a valuable member of a fishing crew, responsible for feeding the men and, in the case of the fishing schooners, handling the boat while the rest of the men fished. Because of this added responsibility, a good cook was paid a larger share than the rest of the crew. Flo Mills was one of the most famous cooks in the days of the Gloucester fishing schooners:

Three times a day he prepared food for seventeen men. . . . Flo Mills kept the pot boiling on the ship. He pared buckets of potatoes, sliced turnips, chopped cabbage, baked huge loaves of bread, cooked meat, baked pies, cookies, and cakes, made puddings and doughnuts, and served seventeen dishes of oatmeal each morning, with coffee too...

He kept the ship in the vicinity of the seine boat; he avoided collisions with other schooners... tacked and turned the Yosemite with as great facility as if he were handling a sloop in Penobscot Bay... sprinting forward to trim the jibs and foresail sheet, darting down to the fo'c'sle... to catch a glimpse of a pie in the oven or a boiling pot, and at last picking up the seine boat without upsetting the boat or tearing the seine.
—Raymond McFarland, *The Masts of Gloucester*

Gingerbread with Lemon Sauce

This gingerbread is spicy and dense. It's great on its own but topped with a generous ladle of warm lemon sauce it is transformed from a leading lady to a movie star. Make the sauce while the gingerbread is in the oven.

Serves 6

FOR THE GINGERBREAD:

8 tablespoons butter, softened

1/2 cup sugar

1 egg, beaten

2 1/2 cups unbleached flour (King Arthur is best)

1 1/2 teaspoons baking soda

1 teaspoon cinnamon

1 teaspoon ginger

1/2 teaspoon ground cloves

1/4 teaspoon salt

1 cup molasses

1 cup hot water

FOR THE LEMON SAUCE:

1 cup sugar

2 tablespoons cornstarch

2 cups boiling water

4 tablespoons butter

1/2 cup fresh lemon juice

1 tablespoon grated lemon zest

To make the gingerbread: Preheat oven to 350°F. In a large bowl cream together the butter and sugar. Add the egg and beat well. In a separate bowl sift together all the dry ingredients; set aside. In a large measuring cup combine the molasses and hot water. Alternately add the molasses and dry ingredients to the butter/sugar mixture, beating well after each addition.

Spoon the batter into a greased 9-inch spring-form pan. Bake for 30–40 minutes, or until a toothpick inserted in the center comes out clean. Cool on a rack for 10 minutes before loosening and removing the sides of the pan. Continue to cool for another 5–7 minutes before cutting into wedges and serving topped with a generous spoonful of warm lemon sauce.

To make the sauce: Combine the sugar and cornstarch in a saucepan. Add the boiling water and mix well. Place over high heat and bring to a boil; cook at a boil for 5 minutes. Remove from the heat and whisk in the butter, lemon juice, and lemon zest. Serve warm.

Blueberry-Lemon Sponge Pie

This dessert is an elegant combination of two old-fashioned dishes—blueberry pie and lemon sponge. The blueberry base is gooey and sweet; the lemon sponge top is light and tart. Bake this the same day you plan to serve it.

Makes one 9-inch pie

1 Basic Pie Crust, blind-baked (see page 163)

3 cups fresh blueberries

6 tablespoons granulated sugar

3 eggs, separated

7 tablespoons superfine sugar

¼ cup plus 3 tablespoon fresh lemon juice

1 tablespoon grated lemon zest

Preheat oven to 400°F.

Combine the blueberries and granulated sugar in a saucepan. Stir gently with a spoon; do not smash. Place over medium heat and cook just until the blueberries are juicy and bubbling. Set a fine-mesh strainer over a bowl and pour the blueberry mixture into the strainer.

Beat the egg yolks with 4 tablespoons of superfine sugar until the mixture is pale and thick. Gradually beat in the lemon juice and zest.

In a glass bowl beat the egg whites (using clean beaters) until soft peaks form. Gradually add the remaining 3 tablespoons of superfine sugar and beat until the whites are glossy.

Mix one-fourth of the egg whites into the egg yolk/sugar mixture. Gently fold in the rest of the egg whites, a fourth at a time, being careful not to deflate the egg whites.

Place the blueberries in the baked pie shell. Add 2½ tablespoons of the strained juice.

Mound the egg white mixture over the blueberries. Gently spread to cover, all the way to the crust.

Bake in the preheated oven for 15 minutes. Cool thoroughly on a rack before slicing to serve.

Safer Boats for Bigger Risks

Today's fishing boats are built and equipped to withstand more dangerous conditions than earlier boats were. Automatic bilge pumps and alarms, steel hulls, radar, radio, flares, and cellular telephones have all increased a fisherman's safety. But even as the equipment has evolved, one thing has not changed: the physical danger of being at sea. The seas, as the waves are referred to, can still be walls of water so high that no horizon is visible when the boat is in the bottom of the trough, and the winds still blow gale force unexpectedly. If anything, fishermen today expose themselves to rougher and more dangerous weather conditions precisely *because* of the capabilities of the new boats.

Meringues with Fresh Fruit

Meringues are pretty easy to make and add a 'wow' factor to dessert. You can top them with fresh berries, sliced grilled peaches or nectarines, or ice cream and homemade hot fudge sauce.

Makes 6 meringues

3 egg whites

½ teaspoon vanilla extract

¼ teaspoon cream of tartar

¾ cup sugar

1 pint fresh strawberries, cleaned and halved

Whipped cream or vanilla ice cream

Preheat oven to 225°F.

Place the egg whites in a mixing bowl; let stand at room temperature for 30 minutes (this step helps them rise higher and faster). Add vanilla extract and cream of tartar; beat on medium speed until soft peaks form. Gradually beat in sugar, 1 tablespoon at a time, on high until stiff glossy peaks form and sugar is dissolved.

Drop six mounds of meringue onto a parchment paper-lined baking sheet. With the back of a spoon, shape each mound into a 3-inch wide circle with an evenly rimmed dip in the center.

Bake at 225°F for 1–1½ hours or until set and dry. Turn the oven off. Leave the meringues in oven for 1 hour; remove to a cooling rack. When completely cooled, store in an airtight glass or ceramic container (not plastic).

To serve, fill the meringue shells with strawberries and top with a little fresh whipped cream or vanilla ice cream. Serve immediately.

Passion Fruit Mousse

Passion fruit has a lemony yet smooth creamy, fresh flavor. Serve this mousse unadorned, or with a few fresh raspberries on top and a little whipped cream.

1 14-ounce package passion fruit pulp, unsweetened (available in the frozen food section)

1 cup sugar

2 tablespoons fresh lemon juice

2 tablespoons water

1 ½ tablespoons unflavored gelatin

1 cup condensed milk

6 egg whites

In saucepan stir together passion fruit pulp and sugar.

Combine the lemon juice and water in a small bowl and sprinkle the gelatin over it. Let sit for 3 minutes or until softened. Add to the passion fruit and sugar and cook over medium heat until mixture is smooth; do not allow to boil.

Remove from heat; cool completely.

When the mixture is completely cooled, stir in the condensed milk.

In a clean mixing bowl, beat the egg whites until stiff. Stir a third of the egg whites into the cooled passion fruit mixture until combined. Gently fold in the remaining egg whites.

Spoon mousse into footed serving dishes, cover, and refrigerate. Chill for at least 2 hours before serving.

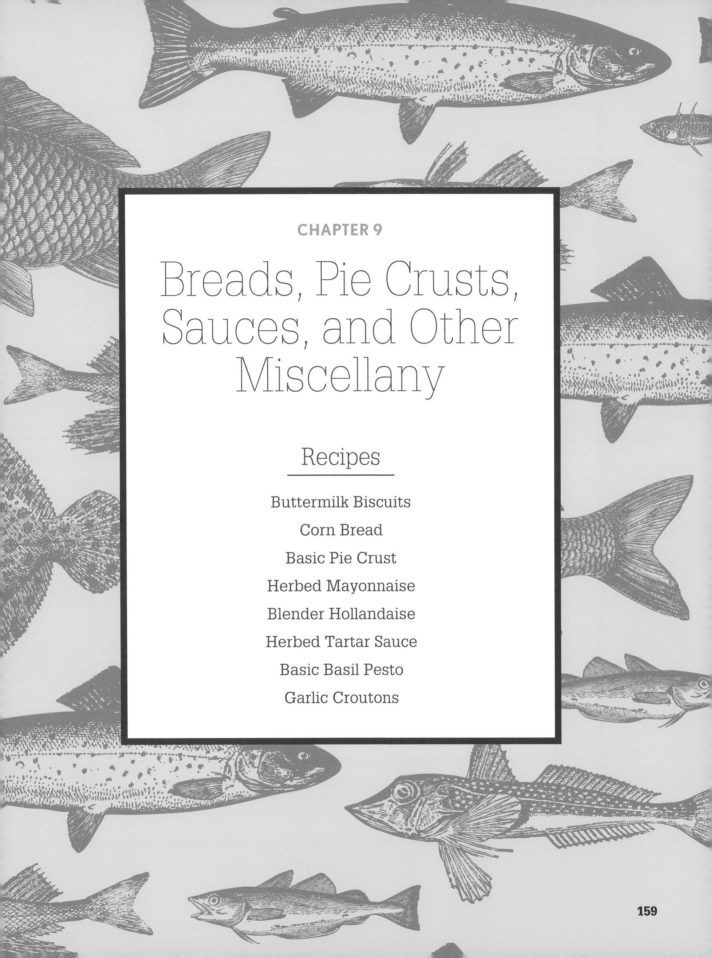

This chapter includes recipes for the staples frequently called for throughout this book. Once you've tried them, you'll turn to them again and again—whether or not you're cooking a seafood meal.

Warm homemade biscuits or bread can change even the simplest supper to something special. Biscuits and cornbread are made with baking powder and baking soda so, unlike yeasted breads, they require no rising time before baking.

I still remember how, as a young girl visiting my Aunt Mabel and Uncle Dennis on their farm in Texas, my aunt made fresh biscuits every morning to serve with eggs from her hens. Those biscuits were so delicious! I'd eat mine split and topped with butter and honey, which would melt almost immediately because the biscuits were hot out of the oven a few feet from the kitchen table. For lunch, leftover biscuits would be split and filled with ham. When I was old enough to think about it, I marveled at Mabel's habit of baking from scratch every morning, even in that Texas heat.

Now, I make fresh biscuits—for breakfast, or dinner—whenever the mood strikes. They are a perennial crowd-pleaser but, as you'll discover, they are easy (and quick) to make. Use a top-quality flour for the best results; I think King Arthur is best.

Pie crust goes together quickly, and if you like, the dough can be made in advance. Wrap it well in plastic wrap and then foil and store in the refrigerator for up to a week or in the freezer for up to a month.

The herbed mayonnaise will keep for about two weeks in the refrigerator, and you'll find it's handy for many uses. Try it on sandwiches, as a dip for fresh vegetables, or thinned with lemon juice as a salad dressing.

Pesto freezes well, so make a batch (or a double batch) whenever fresh basil is in abundance from your own garden or your local farmers' market.

You can make the garlic croutons anytime; they keep well in an airtight glass container at room temperature for a couple of weeks. When I'm at my favorite bakery, I buy an extra loaf of rustic bread just for croutons if my supply is getting low.

One of the secrets to being considered a good cook is having a variety of staples and "special" items at the ready. This small group of recipes will get you started.

Buttermilk Biscuits

Make these according to this recipe until you have them down pat. Then, you can improvise by adding a little cheese—grated cheddar or Parmesan cheese—and/or snipped fresh chives or other herb of your choice.

Makes 1 dozen

3 cups unbleached flour (King Arthur is best)

½ teaspoon salt

1 tablespoon baking powder

8 tablespoons cold butter, cut in chunks

1 cup buttermilk

Fish and the Price of Freedom

Cod fishing was the major industry of the New England colonies and, eventually, became a main source of funding for the American Revolution. Cod was salted, packed in barrels, and shipped to England, which allowed for the purchase of manufactured goods from Europe; those goods were shipped to the West Indies, and from there sugar, rum, and molasses were sent to New England. It was a lucrative triangle of trade. In 1775 the English parliament passed a bill that prohibited the New England colonies from trading directly with foreign countries, and prevented New England vessels from fishing the banks off Newfoundland—the Grand Banks, the richest fishing waters in the western world. Among other deleterious effects, these laws meant ruin to the New England fish-curing industry and added impetus to the other factors that sparked the Revolutionary War.

Preheat oven to 425°F.

Place the flour, salt, and baking powder in a food processor fitted with the plastic blade and pulse once to combine.

Add the butter and pulse until the mixture resembles coarse meal. Add the buttermilk and pulse just until the dough leaves the sides of the bowl.

Turn the dough out onto a lightly floured board. Flour your hands and knead and pat the dough into a smooth ball. Flatten it slightly with your hands. Dust a rolling pin with flour and, working from the center of the ball and rolling outward, flatten the dough to a generous ¾- to 1-inch thickness.

Cut the dough with a biscuit cutter and place on an ungreased cookie sheet. Bake for 10–12 minutes; they should be tall and a light golden tan color on top, and will pull apart easily into a perfect top and bottom. A toothpick inserted in the side that comes out clean tells you they are done. Serve hot.

Corn Bread

For best results bake this bread in a cast-iron skillet.

Makes one 10-inch round

1 cup yellow cornmeal

1½ cups unbleached flour (King Arthur is best)

½ teaspoon salt

2 teaspoons baking soda, sifted

2 eggs

1 cup buttermilk

2 tablespoons maple syrup

8 tablespoons melted butter, divided

Preheat oven to 400°F.

Combine the cornmeal, flour, salt, and baking soda in a large bowl. In a separate bowl beat the eggs; add the buttermilk, maple syrup, and 4 table-spoons (¼ cup) melted butter and beat well. Pour the wet ingredients into the dry and mix well.

Add the remaining ¼ melted butter to the skillet and set over medium heat. When the butter is siz-zling hot, quickly pour in the batter, using a rubber spatula to scrape all the batter out of the bowl and into the skillet. Turn off the heat and place the skillet in the preheated oven.

Bake for 20 minutes or until the top of the corn bread is golden and crisp, and the sides have pulled away from the edges of the pan. Cool for 5 minutes before cutting into wedges to serve.

Try one of these variations:

Add 1 cup of fresh corn kernels to the batter.

Top with ½ cup grated long-horn cheddar cheese halfway through the baking process.

Add 3 tablespoons chopped fresh chives to the batter.

Add 1 finely chopped jalapeño pepper to the batter.

A common expression among fishermen: "The worst day fishing still beats the best day working."

Basic Pie Crust

This basic pastry recipe is fine as is but it can be modified. Add three tablespoons of grated Parmesan cheese when making a crust for a savory dish; add a tablespoon of sugar when it will be used for a dessert. You can also add small amounts of spices or dried herbs. Always chill the dough for at least thirty minutes before rolling it out.

Blind-baking (directions follow) prevents the crust from becoming soggy when filled.

Makes one 9-inch crust

1¼ cups unbleached flour (King Arthur is best)

⅛ teaspoon salt

8 tablespoons cold butter, cut in pieces

1 tablespoon fresh lemon juice

2 or 3 tablespoons cold water

Place the flour, salt, and butter in a food processor fitted with the plastic blade and pulse until the mixture resembles coarse meal. (Or place in a large bowl and cut in the butter using a pastry cutter or two forks.) Add the lemon juice and 2 tablespoons of cold water while the food processor is running. If the dough stays together when pinched, you do not need to add the rest of the water. If it does not, add another tablespoon of water and pulse briefly. Form the dough into a ball, flatten into a 1-inch thick disk, wrap in plastic wrap, and refrigerate for at least 30 minutes.

When the dough has chilled for at least 30 minutes (or up to 24 hours), roll it out on a lightly floured surface to a thickness of about ⅛ inch and use to line a pie plate or tart pan. Cover with plastic wrap and chill for 30 minutes to 1 hour before filling and baking, or blind-baking.

How to blind-bake a pastry shell: Preheat the oven to 425°F.

Line a pie plate or tart pan with rolled pastry dough and prick the bottom all over with a fork. Gently place a sheet of foil over the pricked dough and weight it down with ½ cup of dried beans, rice, or pastry weights.

Bake for 15 minutes. Remove the weights and foil and bake for an additional 3–5 minutes, or until the crust is a very pale gold color. Remove to a cooling rack and let cool completely before you fill it.

Tarts vs. Pies

Unlike pie plates, tart pans are two pieces: a bottom and a fluted side. Tarts are also thinner than pies and do not have a top crust, as some pies do.

When making a tart, always place the tart pan on a cookie sheet before lining it with pastry and filling. That way you have the cookie sheet to hold on to as you put the tart in the oven and, later, take it out. Drape the rolled pastry dough over the pan and loosely fit the dough in place. Trim the excess, leaving a half-inch overhang. Fold the overhang to the inside of the tart pan, creating a double layer of dough at the fluted edge. Gently press the double layer together and into the sides of the pan so that the two layers become sealed and the fluted edge of the pan shapes the dough. The dough will be slightly higher than the top edge of the tart pan. Gently and slowly roll a long rolling pin across the top of the tart pan, starting at the center and rolling out, once in each direction. Pull away any dough that has been "trimmed" by the rolling pin.

After baking, carefully slide the tart pan off the cookie sheet and onto a cooling rack. When the tart has cooled completely, place your hand under the bottom to lift it up and away from the fluted ring (the side of the pan). Now, you can see the beautiful fluted edge. Transfer to a serving plate.

Herbed Mayonnaise

This mayo is made in a blender, and the results are wonderful. Use it as a dip for chilled shrimp cocktail or marinated jumbo shrimp hot off the grill. It goes nicely with lots of other seafood too—grilled tuna, monkfish, and swordfish, to name a few.

Make it in advance because it needs to chill for a couple of hours. It will keep, refrigerated in a glass jar, for up to two weeks.

Makes about 2 cups

4 garlic cloves, peeled

1 egg, plus 2 egg yolks

2 tablespoons fresh lemon juice

1 teaspoon salt

1¼ cups extra-virgin olive oil (best quality)

1 cup packed fresh herbs: cilantro, basil, parsley, dill, or a combination of your choice

¼ teaspoon cumin (optional)

Place the garlic in a blender and process. Add the egg, egg yolks, lemon juice, and salt, and blend well. Slowly pour in the olive oil in a thin stream while the blender is running (do this through the hole in the lid). Continue blending until the mixture is thick. Add the herbs and cumin (if using), and process thoroughly. Pour into a clean glass jar, cover tightly, and refrigerate for at least 2 hours.

To use as a salad dressing, mix a little lemon juice and/or buttermilk with a portion of the mayonnaise. Thin to desired consistency.

CILANTRO DRESSING:

1 cup prepared Herbed Mayonnaise (made with cilantro)

1 tablespoon fresh lemon juice

1 tablespoon buttermilk

Whisk together all ingredients. Use immediately.

Blender Hollandaise

This delicious lemony sauce is made in a blender in no time. Add the herb of your choice. The butter must be piping hot, and you should only make this sauce right before using it. Try it on a smoked salmon and eggs Benedict, or on crab cakes, broiled oysters, cold lobster—you get the picture!

Makes about 1 cup

3 egg yolks

3 tablespoons fresh lemon juice

8 tablespoons butter, melted and piping hot

¼ teaspoon freshly ground pepper

1 tablespoon chopped fresh herbs: dill, parsley, basil, tarragon, or chives

Place the egg yolks and lemon juice in a blender and process on high for 2 minutes. The mixture should be pale yellow and greatly increased in volume.

With the blender running, add the piping hot butter in a slow stream (through the hole in the blender lid). Continue to process until the mixture reaches the desired thickness. Add the pepper and herb of your choice and process briefly. Use immediately.

Fishing—the Most Dangerous Job

According to the U.S. Census Bureau, the Bureau of Labor Statistics, and the Office of Merchant Marine Safety, commercial fishing is the most dangerous occupation in the United States—far more hazardous than coal mining, which is the most dangerous of land occupations.

Herbed Tartar Sauce

Serve this sauce with fish and chips, pan-fried scallops, crab cakes, grilled tuna steaks, or any other seafood, really. It's also great as a spread for sandwiches made with leftover pan-fried fish. Use your favorite herb.

Makes about 2 cups

1½ cups mayonnaise

2 tablespoons minced shallots

3 tablespoons finely chopped fresh herb: basil, tarragon, dill, or flat leaf parsley

3 tablespoons minced cornichons (small French pickles)

1 tablespoon fresh lemon juice

¼ teaspoon paprika

In a small bowl combine all ingredients well. Store in the refrigerator in an airtight glass container. Keeps for a few days.

Basic Basil Pesto

Basil pesto is handy for pizza, pasta, salads, and baked or grilled fish. I make two batches at a time, and store a little in the fridge and the rest in the freezer in 1-cup containers.

Makes about 2 cups

2½ cups packed fresh basil leaves

4 garlic cloves

1 cup walnuts or pine nuts

¾ cup extra virgin olive oil (best quality)

1 cup grated Parmesan cheese

1 tablespoon fresh lemon juice

Salt and freshly ground black pepper to taste

Place the basil, garlic, and nuts in a food processor fitted with the metal blade and pulse until the mix is finely chopped. Add the oil in a stream through the feed tube with the processor running. Add the cheese, lemon juice, and a little salt and pepper. Pulse briefly. Transfer to an airtight container and store in the refrigerator or freezer. Keeps in the refrigerator for a week or in the freezer for up to a month.

Variation: Substitute baby arugula leaves for half of the basil.

Garlic Croutons

You'll need these croutons for Caesar salad, of course, and a number of recipes in the Seafood Salads chapter. They are also good sprinkled on soup.

Makes about 8 cups

1 large loaf of Italian or other rustic bread (12 ounces)

4 tablespoons olive oil

4 tablespoons butter

4 garlic cloves, peeled and scored

Trim the crust off the loaf (save the crust for homemade breadcrumbs), and slice the loaf in ½-inch slices; cut the slices into cubes. If the bread is fresh, spread the cubes on a cooling rack to sit for half a day to dry out.

In a 12-inch cast-iron skillet heat 2 tablespoons of the oil and 2 tablespoons of the butter over medium heat. Add 2 cloves of garlic. When the oil is hot, add half of the bread cubes, tossing quickly so that all are coated evenly with the oil/butter mixture. Cook the bread over medium heat, tossing often, until it is golden. Transfer to a cookie sheet lined with brown paper to drain and cool.

Repeat with the rest of the ingredients.

When the croutons have cooled completely, discard the garlic cloves and store the croutons in an airtight glass container. If the croutons are not crisp enough, put them on a large baking pan and place them in a 350°F oven for about 15 minutes, tossing every 5 minutes. Cool on a rack.

Appendices

How to Fillet a Fish

Purchasing Guide

Seafood and Good Nutrition

Nutritional Information Chart

How to Fillet a Fish

Most fish at your local market is available as fillets. But at a good fish market—particularly one near a fishing port—you will also find whole fish on display, such as bluefish, striped bass, mackerel, tautog, sea bass, and sea trout, depending on the time of year. Knowing how to fillet a whole fish will allow you to choose from a greater variety. You will pay less per pound, and you can use the fish carcass to make fish stock.

These are basic directions and illustrations that will work for *most* fish (working with a flat fish like flounder is slightly different). The more you practice, the better you will become at it.

Filleting a fish

1. **Always start with a sharp knife!** A classic fish filleting knife has a long flexible blade.
2. **Remove the fins:** Using kitchen shears, cut off all the fins except the tail fin (it makes the fish easier to hold).
3. **Remove the scales:** Hold the fish by the tail, and using a dull knife held at an angle against the skin, scrape toward the head. Do this over the whole body until you can feel with your hands that all the scales are gone and the body is smooth. Work outdoors or in a deep sink because the scales will fly all over the place as they are scraped off.
4. **Clean the fish:** Using the tip of the knife, make an incision from the area under the jaw, along the belly, all the way to the last fin before the tail. Remove and discard the entrails and rinse the fish well under cold running water.
5. **Cut the fillets from the body:** Place the scaled, cleaned fish on a cutting board with the backbone facing you. Make an incision behind the gills, holding the knife at a slight angle, and cut from the top of the head to the bottom until the knife hits bone. Make a similar cut where the body meets the tail. Next, use the tip of the knife to make an incision in the skin along the backbone, from the back of the head to the tail. Holding the head, insert the fillet knife through the incision in the skin at the head end, parallel to and along the backbone, and toward the belly cavity. Move the knife evenly toward the tail, always keeping the knife cutting just above the bones. When you reach the tail fin, the knife will automatically cut through the last bit of meat and sever the fillet from the body. You should have a boneless fillet, with the skin on. Turn the fish over and repeat the process.
6. **Skin the fillet:** Unless you plan to cook the fillet with the skin on, place the fillet, skin side down, on a cutting board. As close to the tail end as possible, make an incision through the meat down to, but not through, the skin. Grip this bit of meat and skin with one hand and with your other hand hold the knife pressed firmly at a 45-degree angle to the cutting board. Use your hand holding the tail end of the fillet to tug and wiggle the fillet toward the blade of the knife. This motion will cleanly remove the skin from the meat. When you are done, you should have a skinless fillet. If there are still bits of skin adhering to the fillet, carefully cut them off with the knife. If there are any "pin" bones in the fillet, remove them by cutting a v-shaped incision to remove them, or pull them out with tweezers. Save the skin and any other fish parts for stock (store in a sealed bag in your freezer).

Clean fillets

Purchasing Guide

When buying whole fish, look for clear, bulging eyes and bright red gills.

Fresh fish—whole or fillets—should have hardly any odor at all, and what odor there is should be pleasant. The meat should be firm and elastic, and fillets should be moist and gleaming. Whole fish or fillets should be free from slime.

When you visit a fish market, never hesitate to ask questions. This is a good way to learn more about what's available, what's "in season," and whether its season is about to end or is just beginning.

Nowadays most fish is available year-round because the boats are able to go farther afield and in worse weather than ever before. You will notice, however, that seafood prices change throughout the year; that fluctuation is based on supply and demand, and the season. The best way to purchase fresh seafood—at its best and for a good price—is to visit your fish market regularly and discover the specific "seasons" and price cycles for your area.

Clam Sizes

Fresh clams sold in the shell are divided into four size categories: littleneck (the smallest), topneck, cherrystone, and quahog (the largest). The smaller the clam, the more tender the meat.

Steamers are thin-shelled clams, generally a uniform size comparable to littleneck clams. They are never served raw but instead are steamed and served with their strained broth and melted butter.

Seafood and Good Nutrition

Doctors and nutritionists have been advising us for years now to eat seafood more often because of its healthful Omega-3 oils and low-calorie/high-protein profile.

Omega-3 acids raise the levels of HDL (good) cholesterol and can reduce the risk of heart disease and stroke. The American Medical Association released the results of a series of studies in 1995 showing that eating one serving a week of fish high in Omega-3 fatty acids could reduce the risk of heart attack by 50–70 percent. Omega-3 is also beneficial to brain and skin health.

While all seafood contains Omega-3 fatty acids, some has more than others. It is found in highest concentration in mackerel; herring, salmon, anchovies, tuna, bluefish, striped bass, and swordfish are close runners-up. Generally, the oilier or "fattier" the fish, the higher the Omega-3 content.

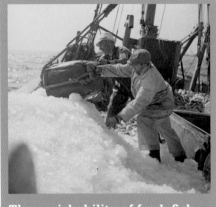

The perishability of fresh fish, and fluctuations in its value, combine to challenge fishermen both at sea and ashore.

There's a lot of confusing information about cholesterol floating around these days. And because certain seafood, particularly lobster, shrimp, and squid, contains higher levels, it's important to be able to sort out the facts. Here's what you need to know: The body needs cholesterol to survive. The cholesterol present in food is *not* what causes high cholesterol levels in the body—fat is. Saturated fat is primarily responsible for increasing blood cholesterol, and all seafood is low in saturated fat (the three previously mentioned contain less than 1 gram per serving).

According to the Washington, D.C.-based Center for Science in the Public Interest, seafood represents one of the best choices for a healthy diet. "Bake, it, broil it, blacken it, grill it—as long as you don't fry it," said Jayne Hurley, the group's senior nutritionist. The National Fisheries Institute, a seafood trade organization, responded to the Center's findings with agreement except on the warning about fried fish: "Fried items, including fried seafood, can be enjoyed in moderation along with a balanced and sensible diet over the course of several meals or several days."

Seafood is also a good source of many important vitamins and minerals, as you can see in the chart that follows.

Nutritional Information Chart

In this chart the values are based on a 3½-ounce or 100-gram portion (a standard nutritional measurement) of uncooked seafood. It is important to note that the "total" fat gram figures include the Omega-3 fatty acids, so do not add the two together.

	Calories	Protein (grams)	Total Fat (grams)	Omega-3 (grams)	Other Benefits
Bass (Sea)	97	18.43	2	.60	181 IU vitamin A, 218 mg potassium
Bass (Striped)	97	17.73	2.33	.75	3.25 mg B-12
Bluefish	124	20.04	4.24	.77	293 mg potassium
Clams	74	12.77	.97	.14	1 4 mg iron, 96 mg calcium
Cod	82	17.81	.67	.18	342 mg potassium
Crab	87	18.06	1.08	.32	89 mg calcium
Flounder	91	18.84	1.19	.20	1.29 mg B-12, 307 mg potassium
Haddock	87	18.91	.72	.19	1.18 mg B-12, 339 mg potassium
Halibut	110	20.81	2.29	.40	440 IU vitamin A, 9.2 mg niacin
Herring	158	17.96	9.04	1.57	110 IU vitamin A
Lobster	90	18.80	.90	.37	61 mg calcium
Mackerel	205	18.60	13.89	2.30	430 IU vitamin A, 2.1 mg iron
Monkfish	76	14.48	1.52	.20	23 mg magnesium
Mussels	86	11.90	2.24	.44	4 mg iron
Oysters	69	7.06	2.47	.44	6.7 mg iron, 94 mg calcium, 320 IU vitamin A
Salmon	146	21.62	5.95	1.44	7.2 mg niacin, 310 IU vitamin A
Scallops	88	16.78	.76	.20	26 mg calcium
Sea Trout	104	16.74	3.61	.37	290 mg potassium
Shrimp	106	20.31	1.73	.48	3.1 mg iron
Skate	89	19.60	.70	—	.02 mg B-1
Squid	92	15.58	1.38	.49	200 mg potassium, 4 mg vitamin C
Swordfish	121	19.80	4.01	.64	9.7 mg niacin, 245 mg potassium, 2000 IU vitamin A
Tautog	94	18.75	1.57	.41	22 mg calcium, 227 mg potassium
Tilefish	96	17.50	2.31	.43	22 mg calcium, 368 mg potassium
Tuna (Bluefin)	144	23.33	4.90	1.17	8.01 mg B-12, 1856 IU vitamin A, 214 mg potassium
Tuna (Yellowfin)	108	23.38	.95	.22	8.3 mg niacin
Whiting	90	18.31	1.13	.22	60 mg calcium

How to Clean Whole Squid

You can buy cleaned squid (fresh or frozen) at the fish market to save a little time in the kitchen. But you'll pay for this convenience—about three times as much as fresh whole squid. Cleaning squid is easy, and fresh squid is tastier and more tender than frozen. Follow these steps:

1. *Remove the fins:* Holding the squid by the head, grasp the two soft fins and pull them up and away from the body (do not cut); they will pop right off.

2. *Remove the skin:* Grip the thin reddish skin between your thumb and index finger; lift and peel. This is a lot like peeling the label off a bottle. Or scrape the skin off with a dull knife.

3. *Remove the head:* Pull the head away from the body; it will separate naturally.

4. *Clean the body:* With a firm tug, pull the clear plastic-like cartilage out of the body. Rinse the body under cold running water to remove ink.

5. *Trim the tentacles:* Using a sharp knife cut off the tentacles as a whole cluster by slicing about ½ inch above where they are joined to the head, just below the eyes.

   Now the bodies are ready to be cut into rings or stuffed. The tentacles can be left whole or halved lengthwise or chopped, depending on the recipe. If desired, skin the fins and use them, too.

Index

Acknowledgments

This book is a revised edition of one I wrote called *A New England Fish Tale* that was published in 1997. I remain deeply grateful to all the individuals who helped make the original book possible—the scores of fishermen and their families who took time to talk with me about their work; the Rhode Island Seafood Council; the Gloucester Fihermen's Wives Association; the Portland Fishermen's Wives Association; the Women's Fisheries Network; the Cape Ann Historical Society; the Chatham Historical Society; the Block Island Historical Society; the Mystic Seaport Museum; the Historical Society of Stonington, CT; and the National Marine Fisheries Service at Woods Hole Oceanographic Institute.

For her unending enthusiasm to see a new edition of the original book, I thank my agent, Jeanne Fredericks.

Thanks to my entire family—seafood lovers and good cooks, all—for their encouragement and friendship. Particular thanks to my parents, Bob and Nancy Watson: they were my first and best teachers in the kitchen and everywhere else in life, for that matter. Along the way, they taught me that the world is wide and varied and as I progress in my own travels upon it, their influence is with me every day.

Lastly, and with deep affection, thanks to Kevin for giving me something to write about—and something delicious to eat!

About the Author

Martha Watson Murphy is an award-winning writer. She has always been interested in food and the people who bring it to us; her early married years as the wife of a commercial fisherman served as a "graduate school" in seafood cookery. In addition to writing about food, she has worked as a restaurant sous chef, private chef, and cooking school instructor.